Brockville Ontario in Colour Photos, Saving Our History One Photo at a Time

Photography
by Barbara Raué
2016

Series Name:
Cruising Ontario

Book 157: Brockville

Cover photo: 119 King Street East, Page 28

Series Name: Cruising Ontario
Saving Our History One Photo at a Time
in colour photos

Books Available in Alphabetical Order:
Aberfoyle, Acton, Alton, Amherstburg, Ancaster, Arthur, Aylmer, Ayr, Bloomingdale, Brantford, Burlington, Caledon, Caledonia, Cambridge, Clifford, Conestogo, Delhi, Dorchester to Aylmer, Drayton, Drumbo, Dundas, Eden Mills, Elmira, Elora, Essex, Fergus, Guelph, Hagersville, Hamilton, Hanover, Harriston, Hespeler, Jarvis, Kingston, Kingsville, Kitchener, Linwood, Listowel, London, Lucknow, Mono, Mount Forest, Neustadt, New Hamburg, Niagara-on-the-Lake, Oakville, Orangeville, Orillia, Owen Sound, Palmerston, Peterborough, Petrolia, Port Elgin, Preston, Rockwood, Sarnia, Seaforth, Sheffield, Shelburne, Simcoe, Southampton, St. Jacobs, St. Marys, St. Thomas, Stoney Creek, Stratford, Thamesford, Tillsonburg, Waterdown, Waterford, Waterloo, Welland, Wellesley, Windsor, Wingham, Woodstock

Other Books by Barbara Raue

Coins of Gold

Arrows, Indians and Love

The Life and Times of Barbara
Volume 1: Inventions That Have Enhanced My Life
Volume 2: Entertainment That I Have Enjoyed
Volume 3: East Coast Trips
Volume 4: Olympics Have Always Intrigued Me
Volume 5: Wonders of the World
Volume 6: Caribbean Cruises We Have Enjoyed
Volume 7: Animals
Volume 8: Storms and Other Major Disasters in My Lifetime
Volume 9: Wars, Terrorist Attacks and Major Disasters

The Cromwell Family Book

Laura Secord Discovered

Daddy Where Are You?

Montana Series
Book 1: Montana Dream
Book 2: Life on the Montana Frontier
Book 3: Montana to Boston and Back

Visit Barbara's website to view all of her books
http://barbararaue.ca

Table of Contents

Brockville, formerly Elizabethtown, is a city in Eastern Ontario in the Thousand Islands region located on the north shore of the Saint Lawrence River opposite Morristown, New York. It is about halfway between Cornwall to the east and Kingston to the west. It is one of Ontario's oldest European-Canadian communities and is named after the British General Sir Isaac Brock.

This area of Ontario was first settled by English speaking people in 1785, when thousands of American refugees arrived from the American colonies after the American Revolutionary War. They were later called United Empire Loyalists because of their allegiance to King George III. The struggle between Britain and the 13 American colonies occurred in the years 1776 to 1783, and divided loyalties among the people. During the 6-year war, which ended with the capitulation of the British in 1782, many colonists who remained loyal to the crown were subject to harsh reprisals and unfair dispossession of their property by their countrymen. Many Loyalists chose to flee north to the British colony of Quebec. Great Britain opened the western region of Canada (known as Upper Canada and now Ontario), purchasing land from First Nations to allocate to the Loyalists in compensation for their losses, and helping them with some supplies as they founded new settlements. In 1785 the first Loyalist to take up land in Brockville was William Buell Senior, an ensign disbanded from the King's Rangers from the State of New York.

In the 19th century the town developed as a local center of industry, including shipbuilding, saddleries, tanneries, tinsmiths, a foundry, a brewery, and several hotels.

In 1855, Brockville was chosen as a divisional point of the new Grand Trunk Railway between Montreal and Toronto. At the same time, the north–south line of the Brockville and Ottawa Railway was built to join the timber trade of the Ottawa Valley with the St. Lawrence River ship route. A well-engineered tunnel for this railway was dug and blasted underneath the middle of Brockville. The Brockville Tunnel was the first railway tunnel in Canada.

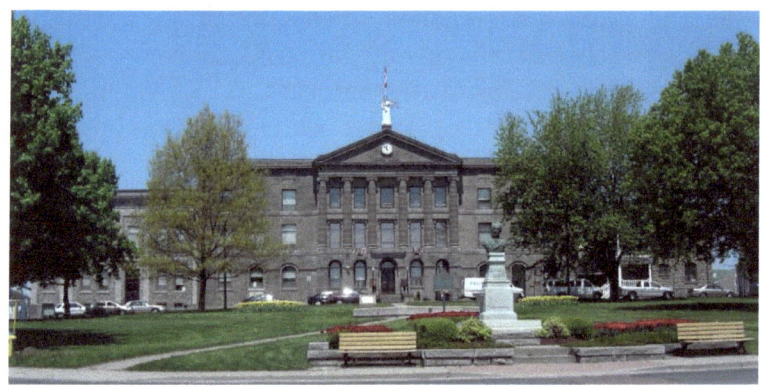

41 Court House Square – District of Johnstown Courthouse
and Gaol – 1843 – Neo-classical style – six pillars with Ionic
capitals, pediment

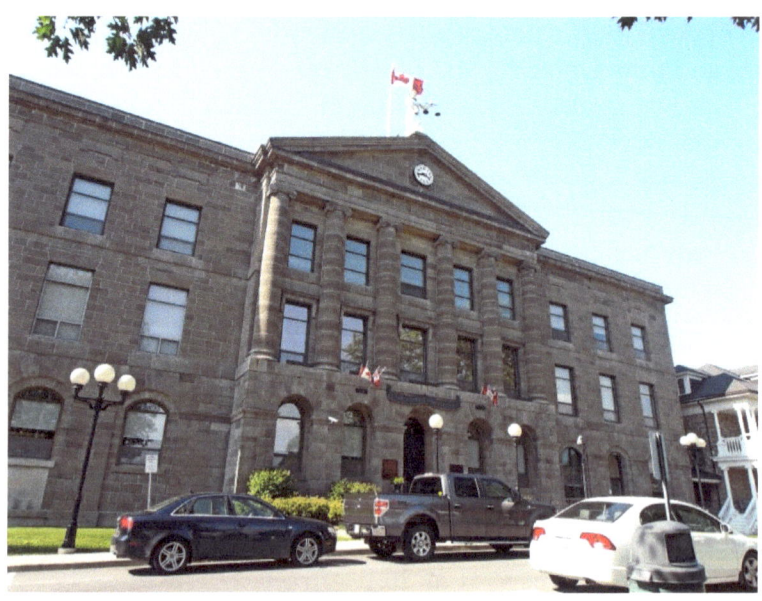

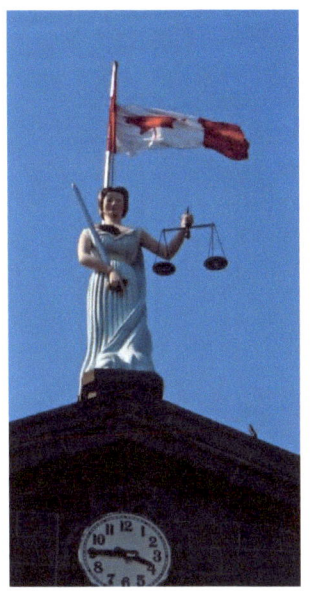
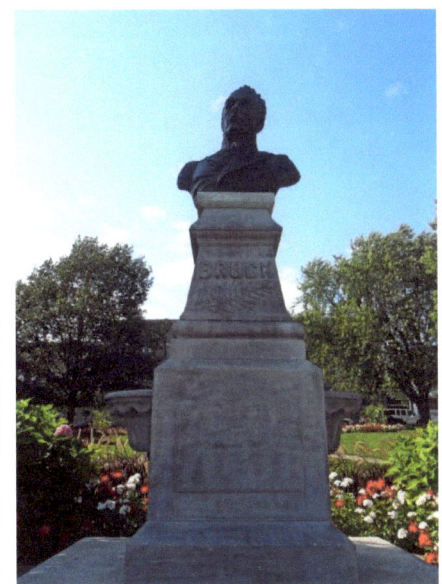

Top of Court House   General Brock Monument - 1912
"Sally Grant" is the familiar name of the Statue of Justice carved by
William Holmes, a Brockville carpenter and builder. The eleven
foot high figure, made of cedar, stood on the roof of the court house
from 1845 to 1956; a replica replaced it in 1981.

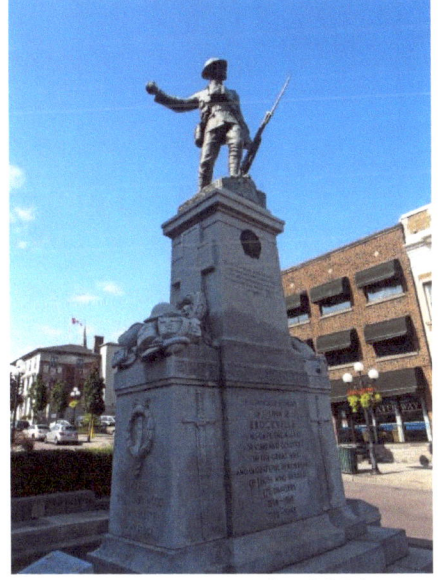

War Memorial - 1924

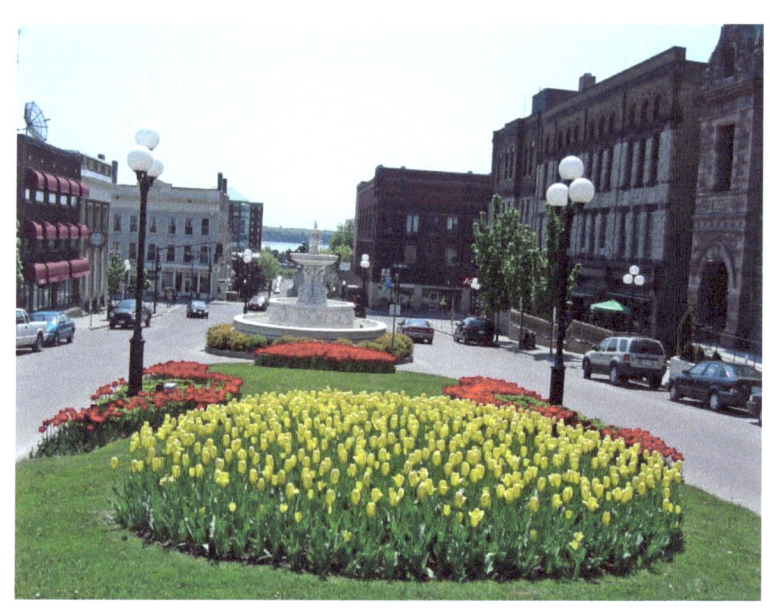

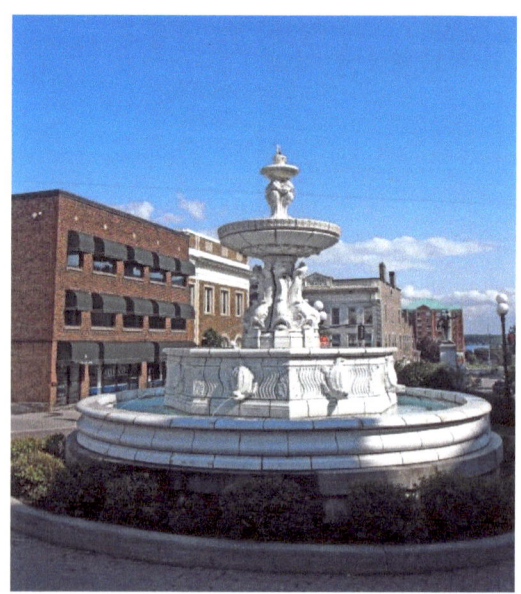

John H. Fulford Memorial Fountain - 1917

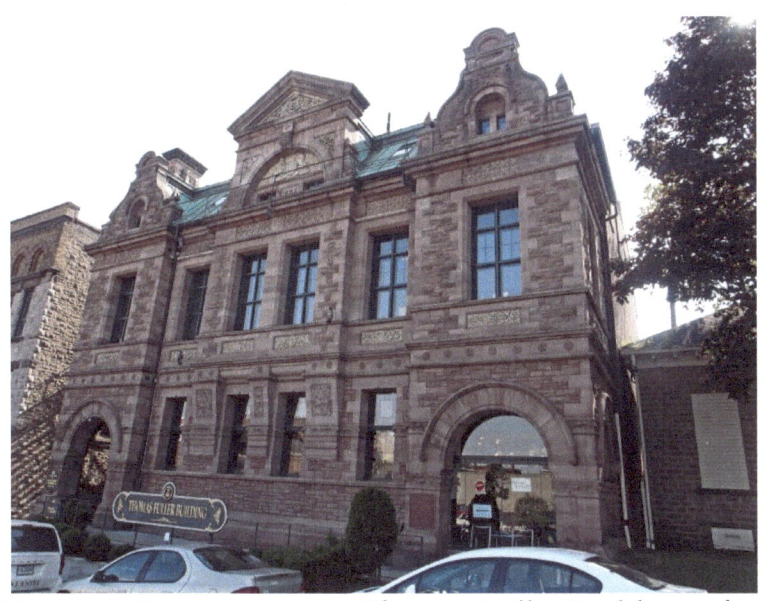

12-14 Court House Avenue – Thomas Fuller Building – former Post Office – 1883-85 - A stone post office, blending Flemish, Queen Anne and Classical elements; a good example of the post offices erected by the Department of Public Works in smaller urban centers during Thomas Fuller's term as Chief Dominion Architect.

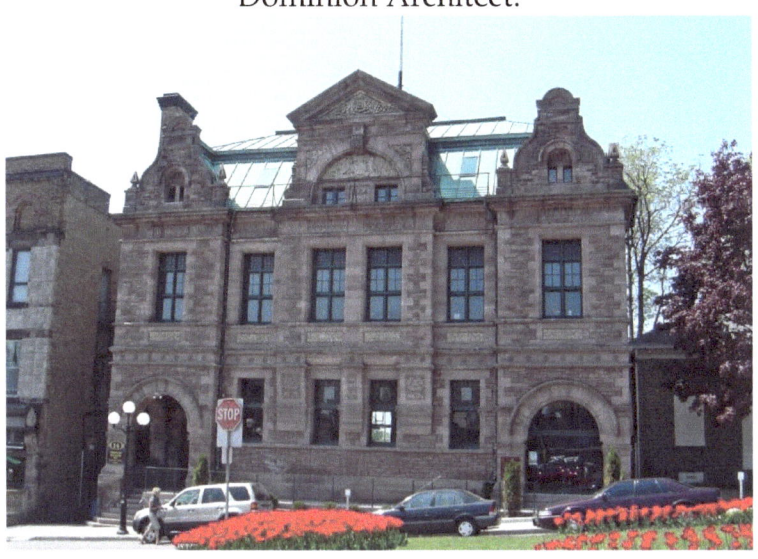

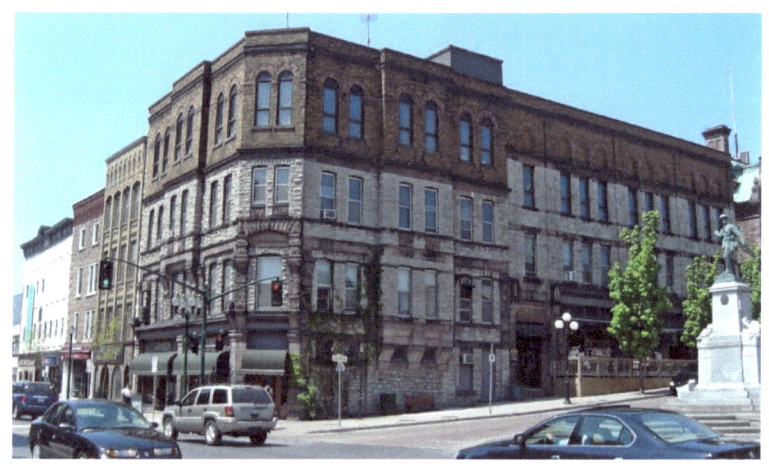

2 King Street West (corner of Court House Avenue) - The Fulford Block – built 1887-1889 – dressed stone front; third floor brick addition with ornate detailing added in 1890s

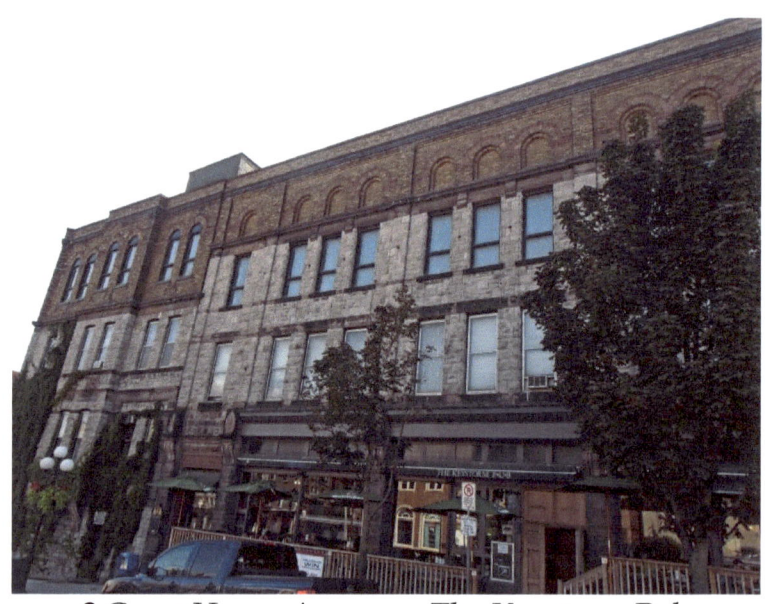

2 Court House Avenue – The Keystorm Pub

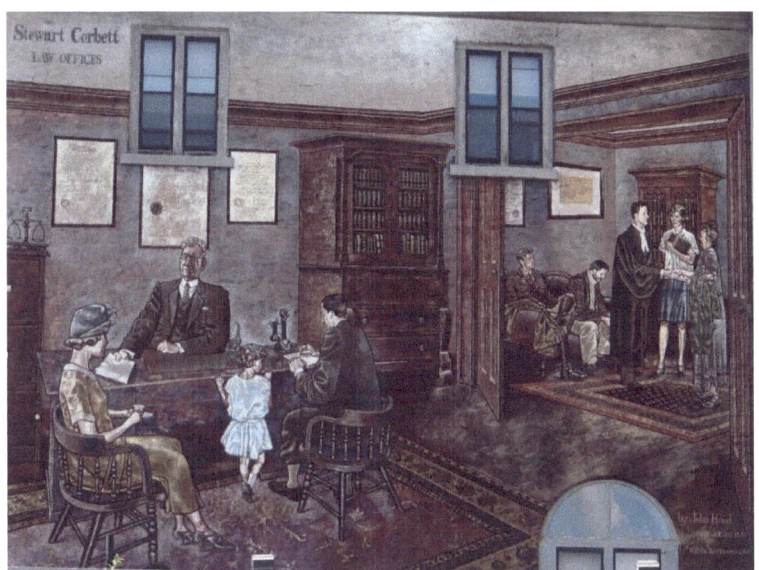

Mural – Stewart Corbett Law Offices

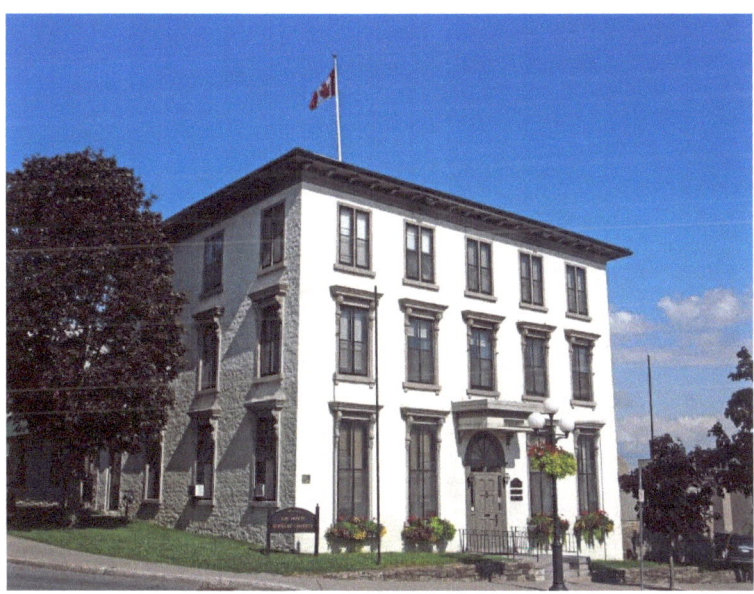

21 Court House Avenue – Hubbell's Building c. 1825 – Law Offices Stewart Corbett – window hoods with cornice brackets, semi-circular transom and sidelights

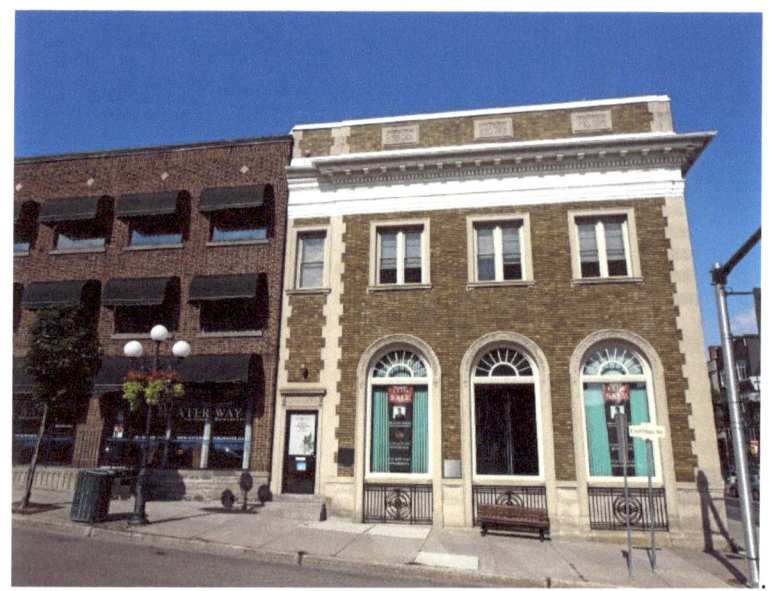

9 Court House Avenue – Waterway Insurance (dark brown building); end building – corner quoins, dentil moulding, decorative brickwork; semi-circular fanlights over three bays

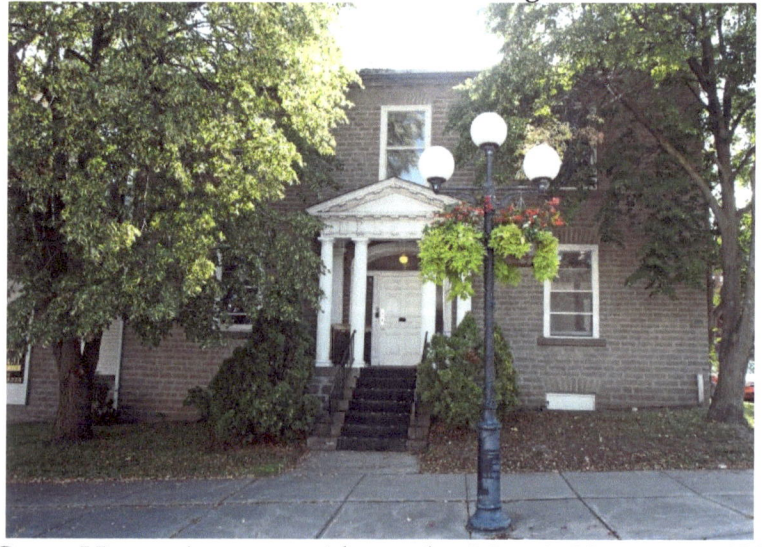

22 Court House Avenue – Alexander Morris House – c. 1835 – Loyalist Neo-classical style; Greek Revival porch with Doric columns supporting pediment

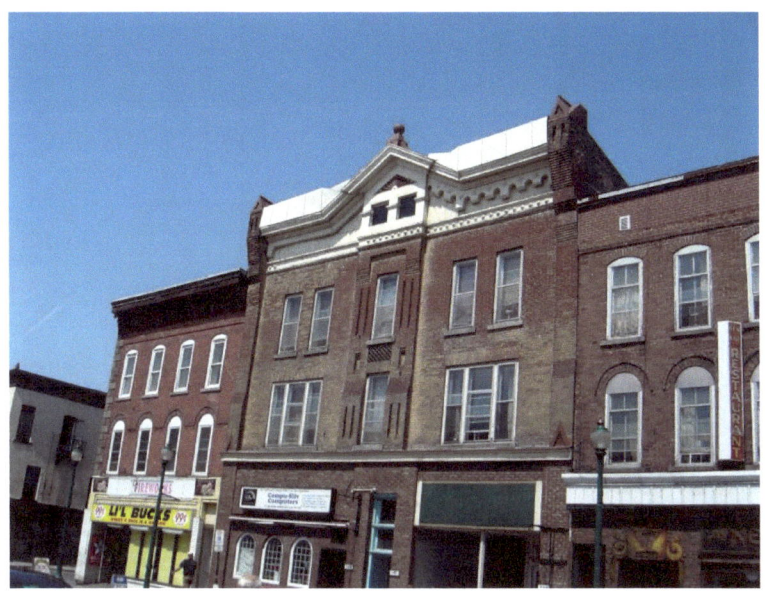

King Street West – pilasters, decorative cornice

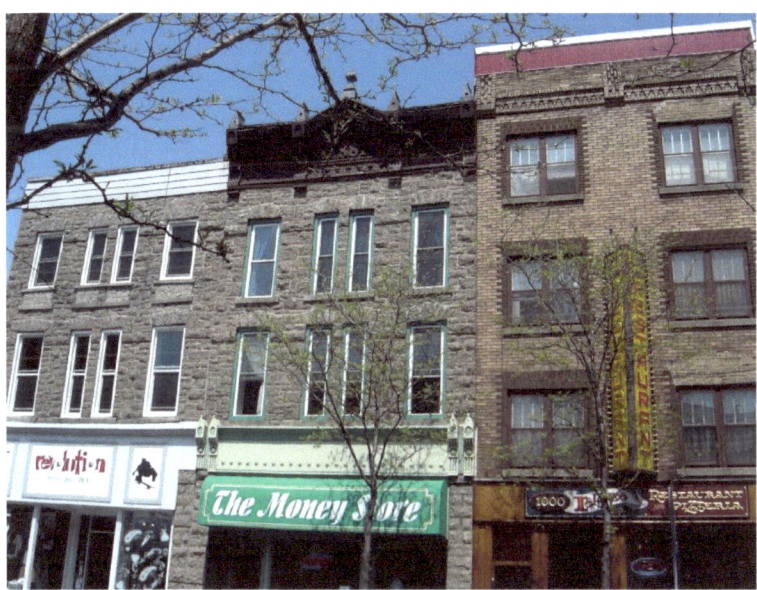

226 King Street West – pediment with date of 1887 and cornice brackets; bevelled dentil molding

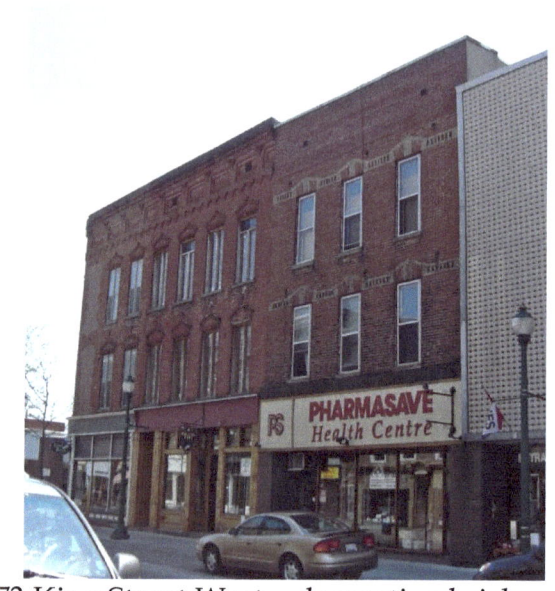

173 King Street West – decorative brickwork

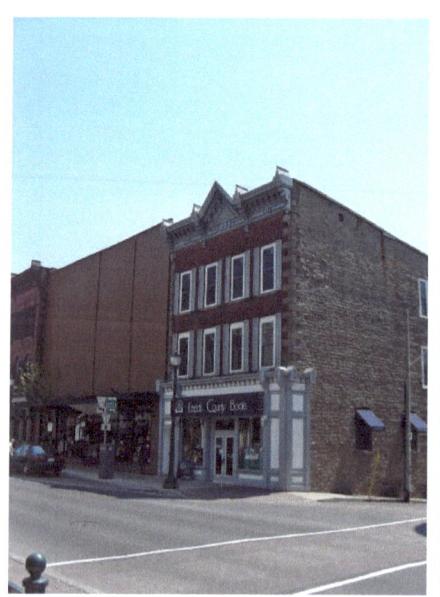
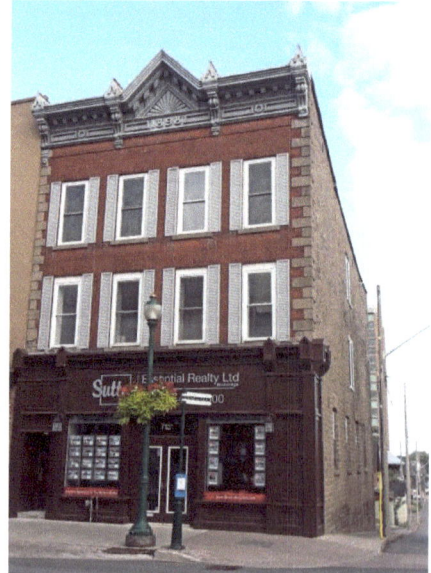

71-73 King Street West - decorative pediment – 1898 –
corner quoins

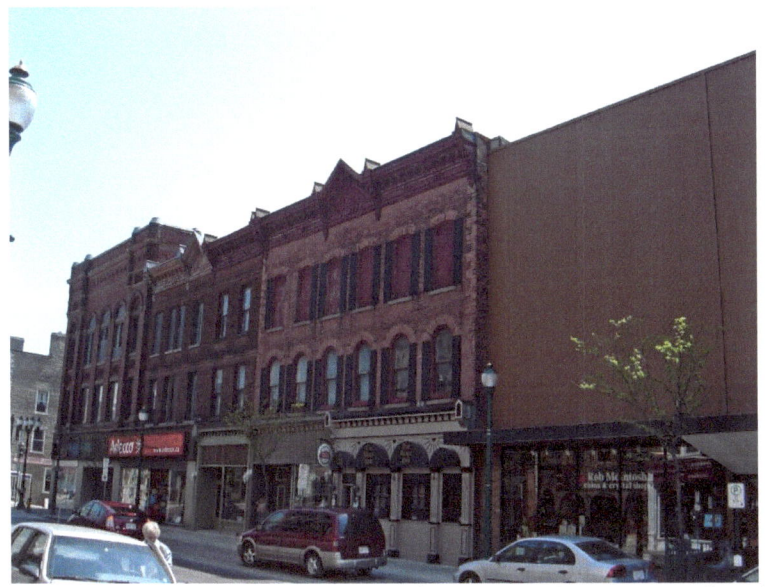

59 King Street West – decorative pediments – 1887; cornice brackets

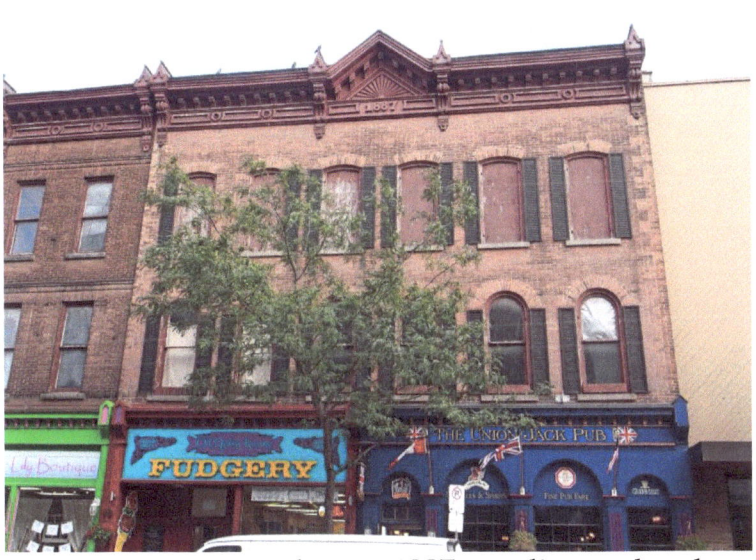

55 King Street West – Fudgery - 1887 – pediment, brackets and decorative cornice, voussoirs

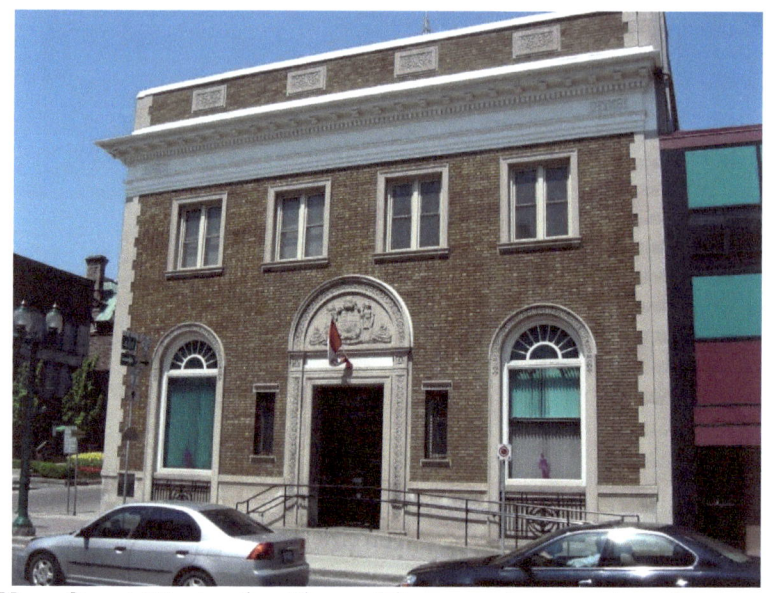

48 King Street West – dentil moulding, quoins, carving above semi-circular transom windows, on semi-circular pediment above door and on panels along sides of door

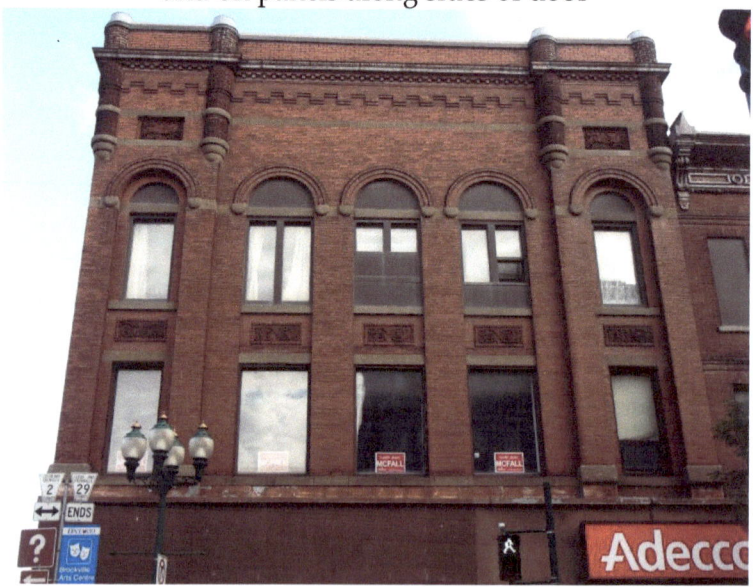

51 King Street West - Dunham Block – 1892 – brick with terra cotta detailing; dentil molding; prominent voussoirs with recessed windows; turrets with corbelling

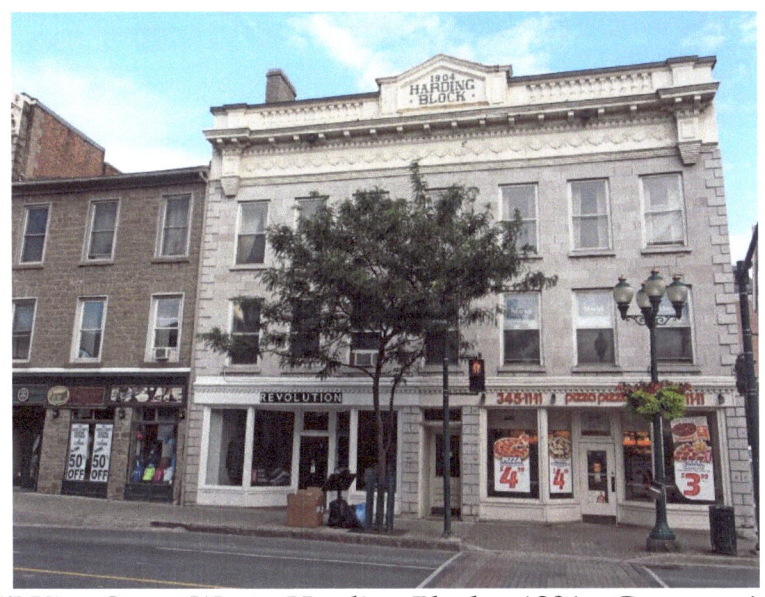

45 King Street West - Harding Block – 1904 – Commercial
Georgian style - decorative cornice, corbels, quoins

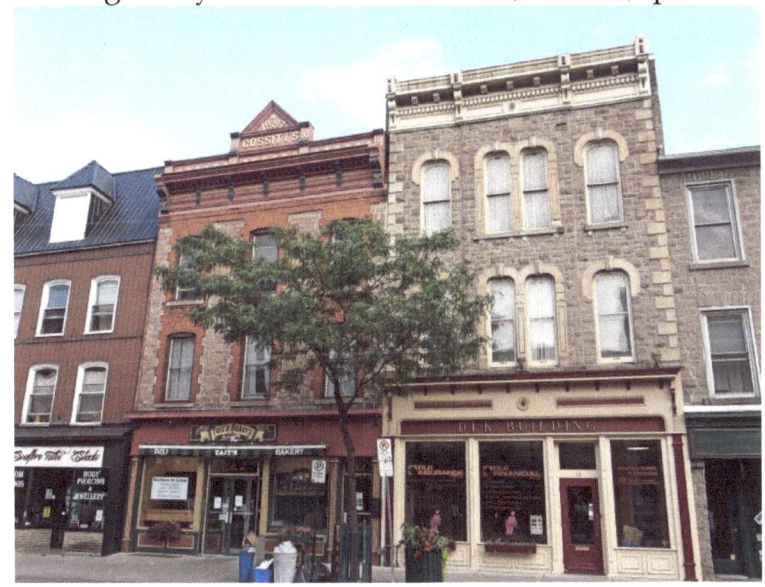

31 King Street West (Tait's Bakery) – Cossitt Building – 1897 –
brick and stone, pediment, cornice brackets
35 King Street West (DLK Insurance) – quoins; cornice
brackets, dentil molding

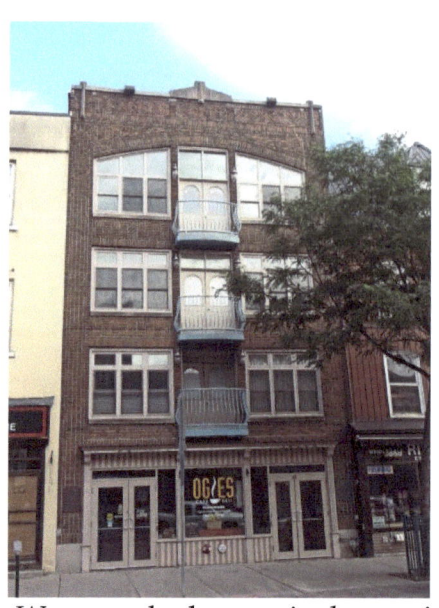

23 King Street West - polychromatic decorative brickwork, balconies

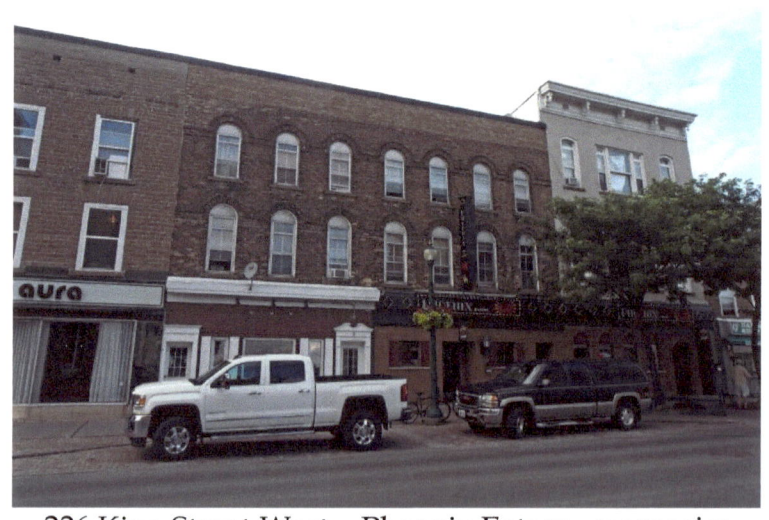

226 King Street West – Phoenix Eatery - voussoirs

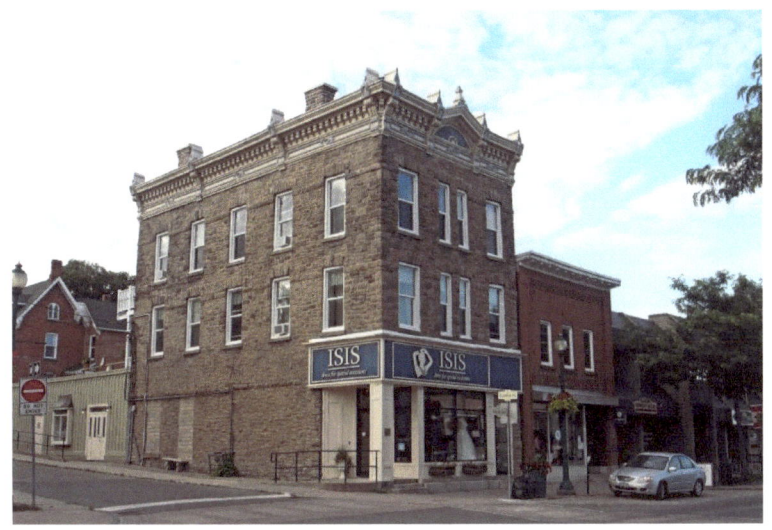

40 King Street West – decorative cornice, brackets, pediment
with sunburst pattern

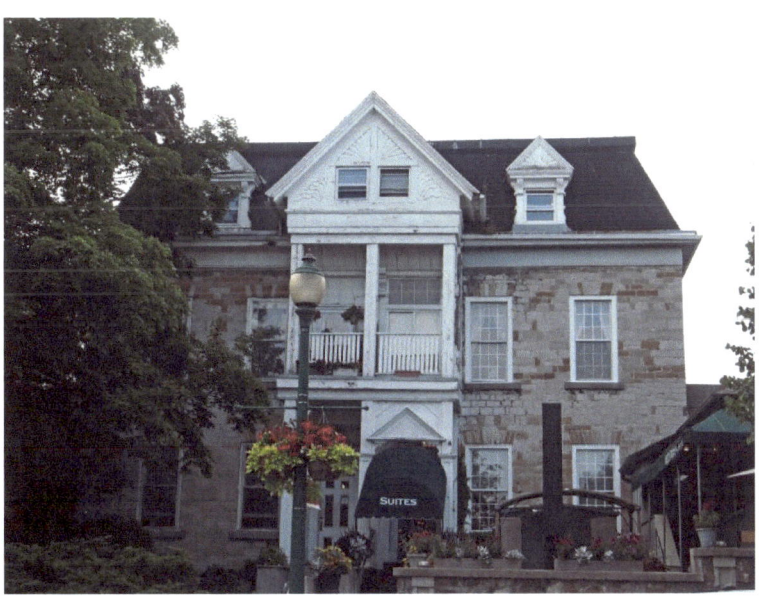

King Street – dormers, gable above second floor balcony

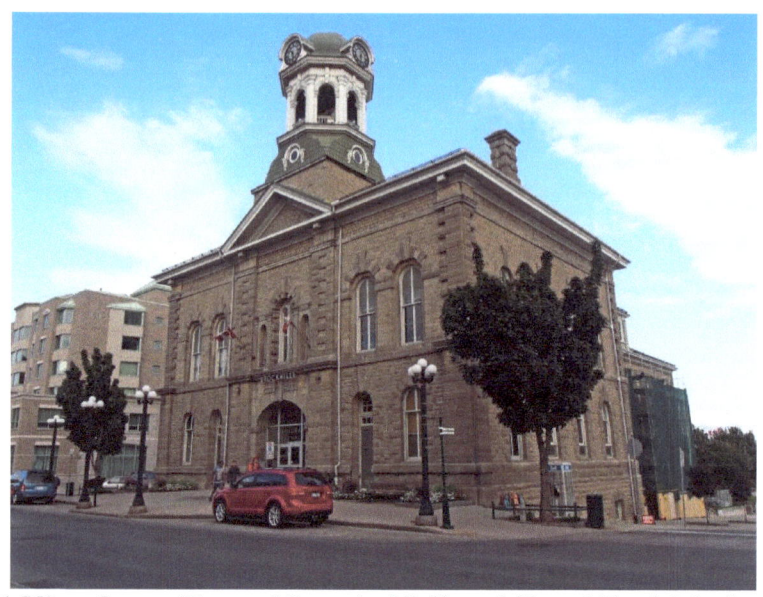

1 King Street East – Victoria Hall and East Ward Market Building – 1863 – designed to show off the success and taste of Brockville s inhabitants – built as a combination concert hall, office space and indoor market house – stone building, intricate detailing, and beautiful clock tower

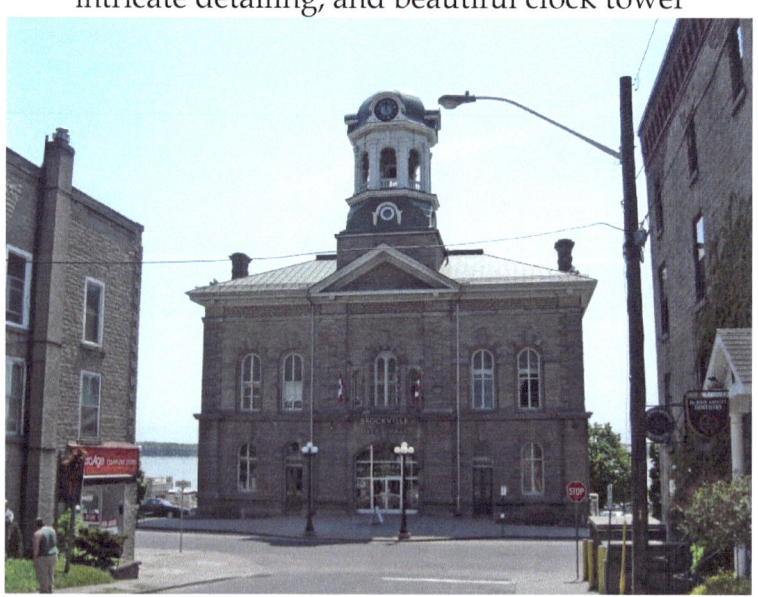

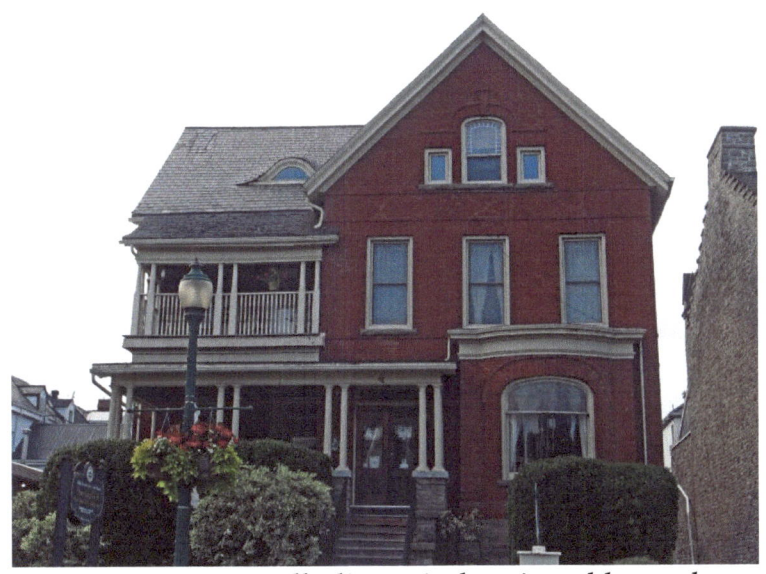

King Street East – Palladian window in gable, eyebrow window in roof, second floor balcony above veranda; bay window

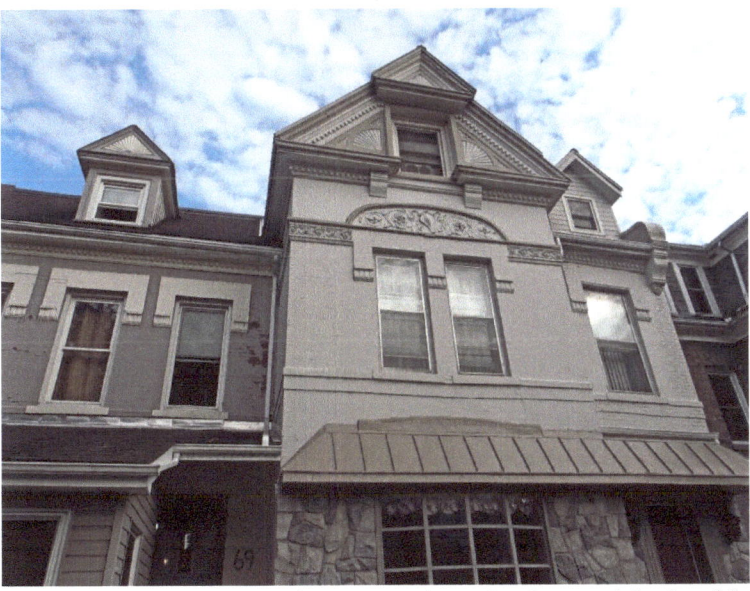

69 King Street East – dormers, frontispiece with double pediment with sunburst patterning and dentil molding, decorative carving above second floor window pair

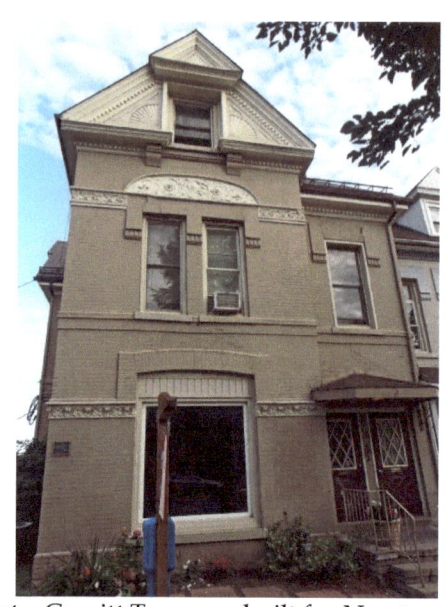

75 King Street East – Cossitt Terrace – built for Newton Cossitt (Architect: George A. Allan) – 1894 - double pediment with sunburst patterning – similar trim to 69 King Street East

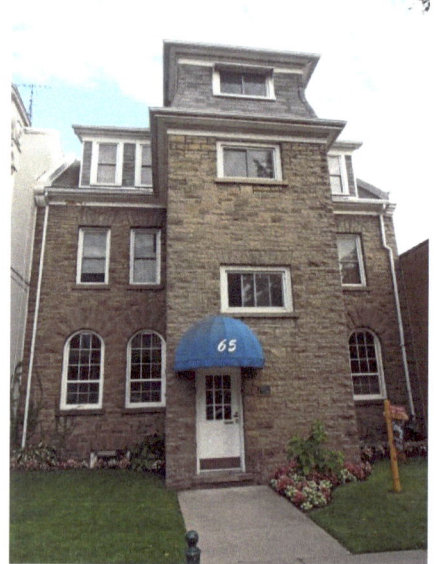

65 King Street East - built as the minister's manse for St. John's Church – c. 1891 – solid stone, four-storey tower, dormers

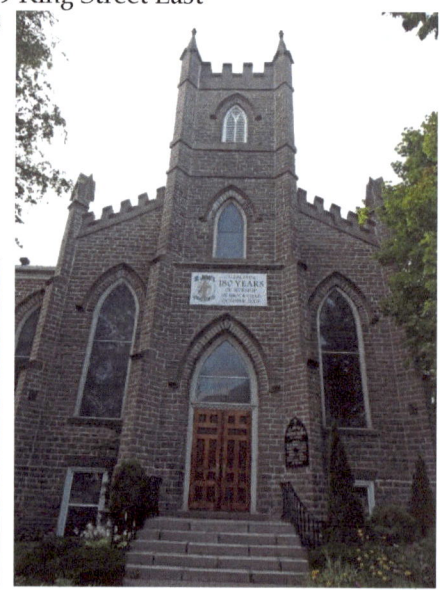

70 King Street East – 1900 - St. John's United Church - Gothic Revival - battlemented parapet, lancet windows

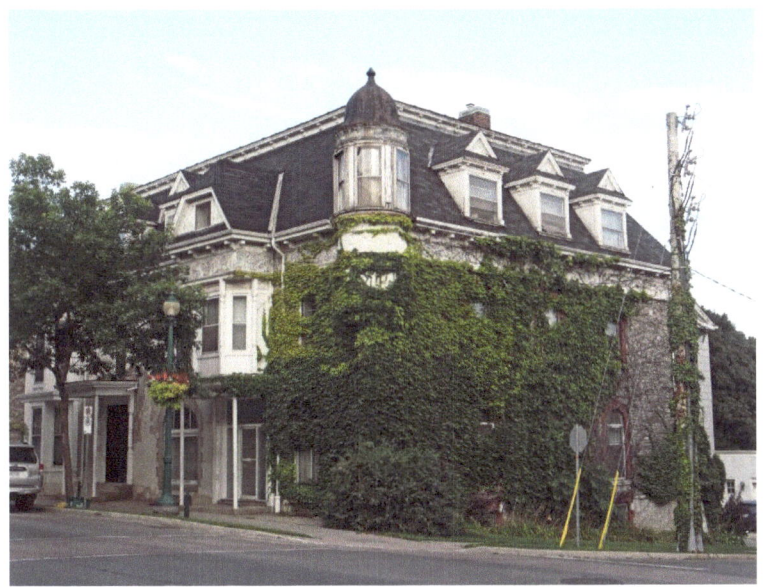

King Street East – c. 1910 - Second Empire style - mansard roof, dormers, turret – homes of the Steacy and Bowie families

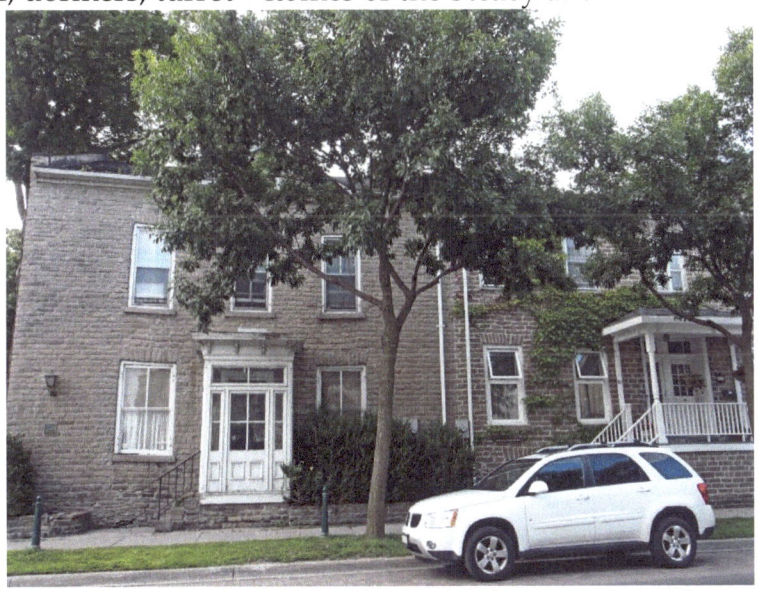

80 King Street East – Paul Glasford House, Merchant – c. 1826; 82/84 King Street East – Eliza Glasford House – c. 1830-1840 – coarse rubble stone

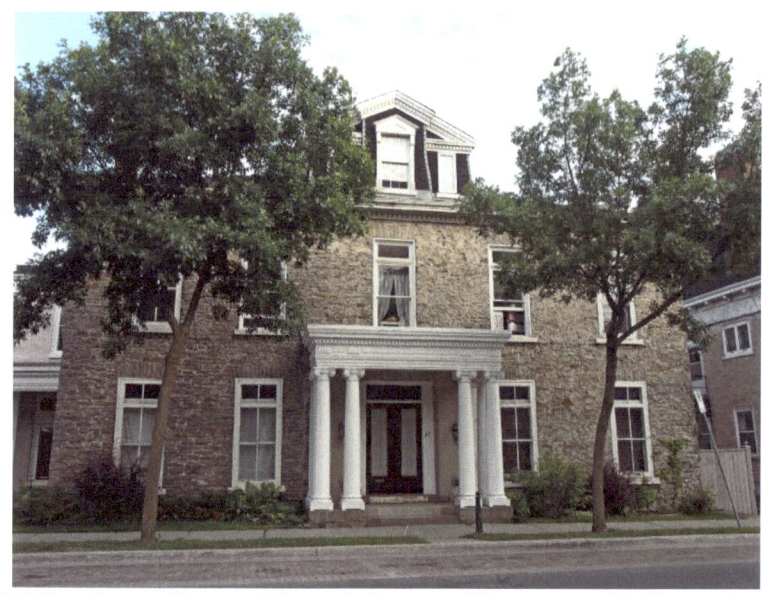

87 King Street East – Edward Kersten House – c. 1847 – stained glass top panel windows on front façade; dormer with pediment with window and hood; Greek Revival style portico supported by six Ionic non-fluted columns and two Ionic pilasters

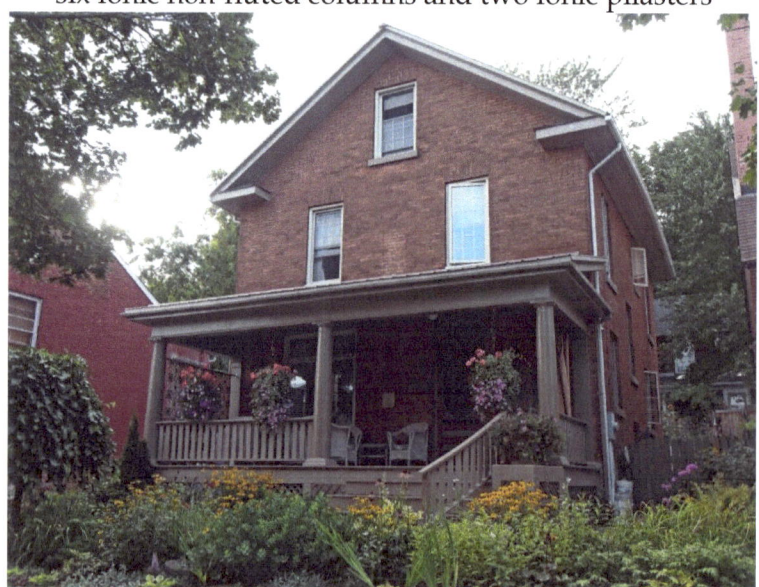

Edwardian - cornice return on gable

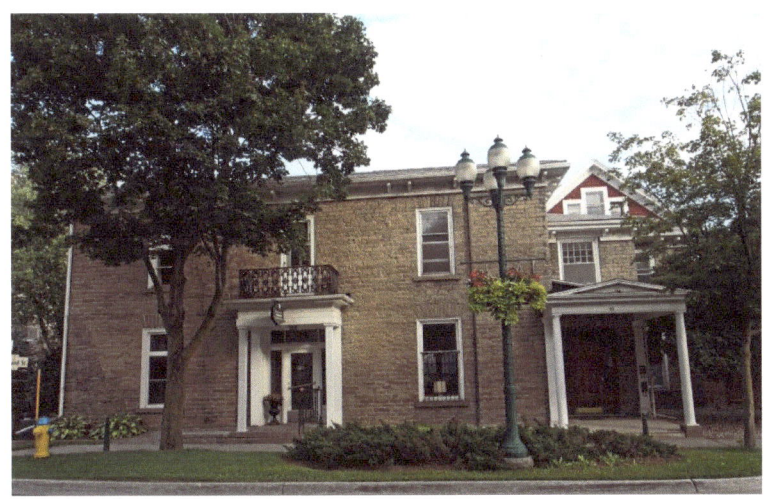

93 King Street East – balcony above one entrance; pediment above other entrance; Palladian window above

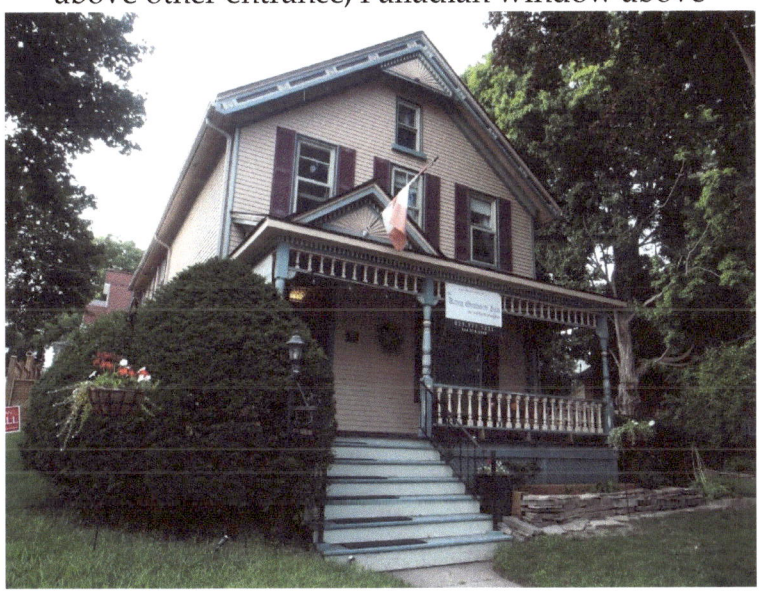

100 King Street East - The King Orchard Inn Bed & Breakfast – Augusta and William Swift House, Insurance Agent – c. 1871 – pediment with sunburst which is repeated at top of gable; wood-turned pillars with spindles under roof of veranda, open railing

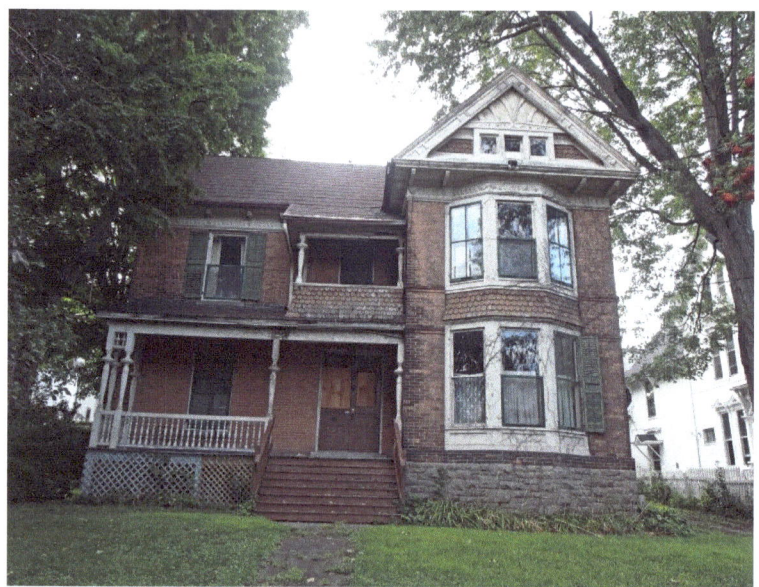

King Street East – two-storey bay window topped with gable;
decorative cornice; balcony with fish scale shingles; wood-
turned spindles supporting veranda with open railing

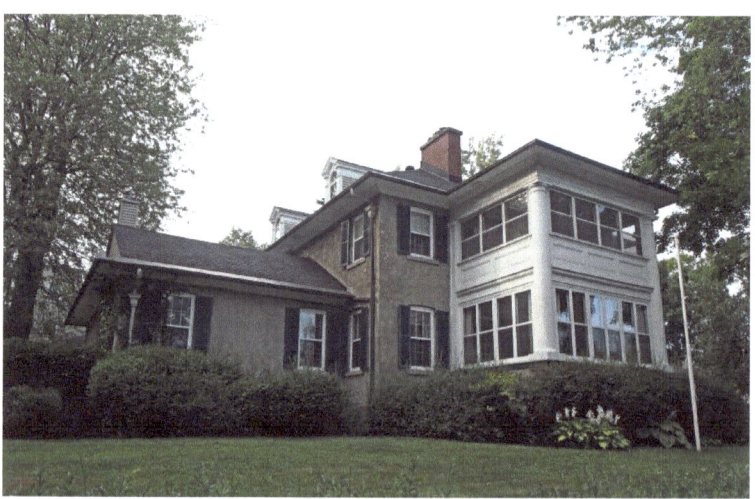

King Street East – dormers, two-storey enclosed porch

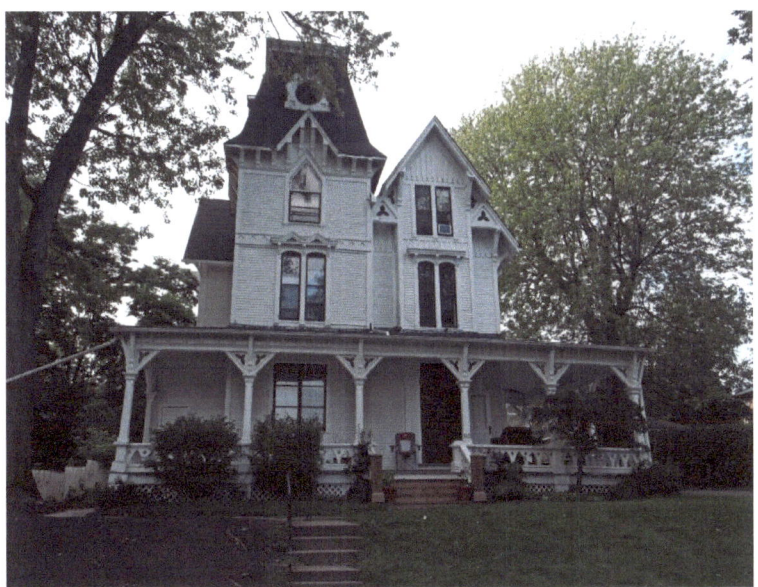

112 King Street East – Alexander Allan House – c. 1880 -Victorian Villa in the Stick Style – irregular in shape, three bays, clapboard sided, four stories, tower, mansard roof, iron cresting, cornice brackets, window hoods, trefoil designs on house and veranda supports

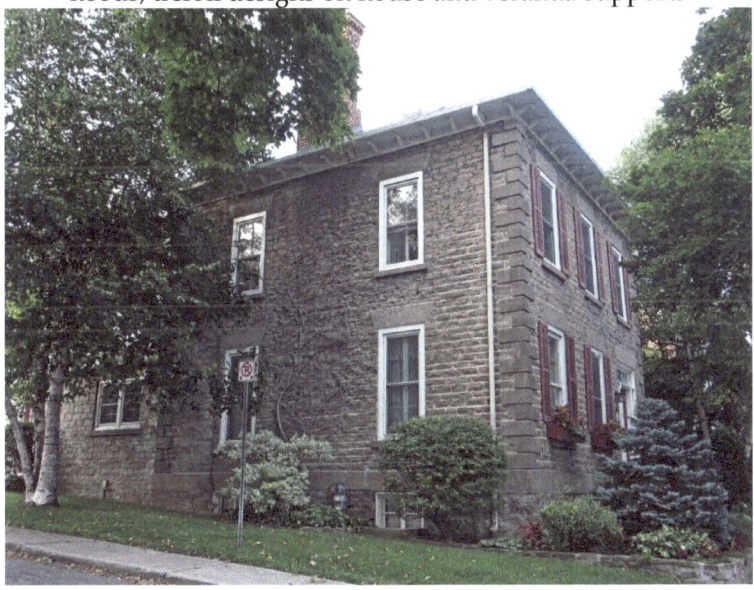

126 King Street East – Thomas R. Sheffield House c. 1863 – Italianate style, hip roof, three bays, off-centre door with sidelights, corner quoins

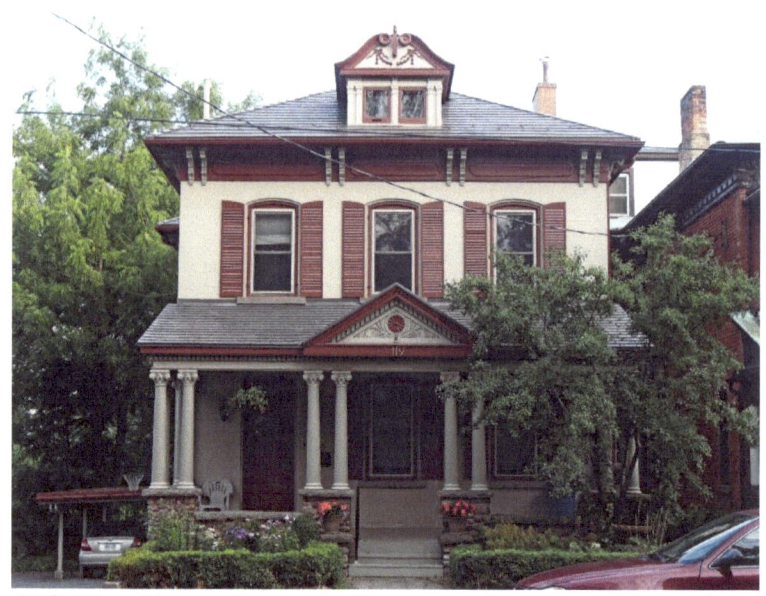

119 King Street East – Italianate - dormer with broken pediment and decorated tympanum; hipped roof; paired cornice brackets; composite pillars supporting veranda with pediment and decorative tympanum

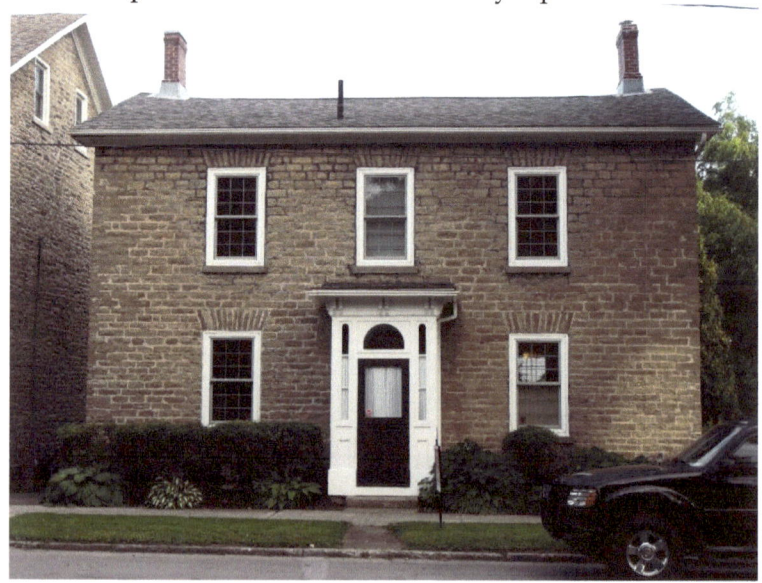

King Street East - voussoirs

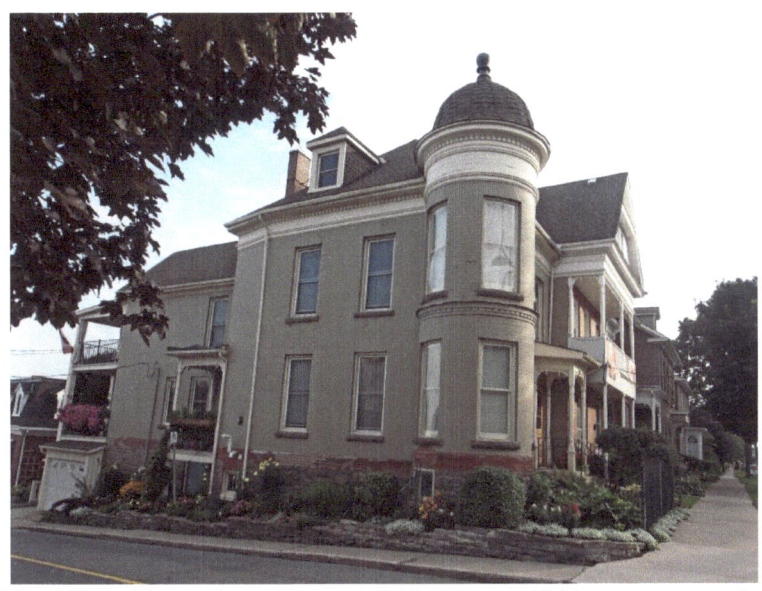

135 King Street East – Brace Terrace (131-135) – c. 1896 - two storey circular
tower; dormer, dentil molding; wood turned porch supports

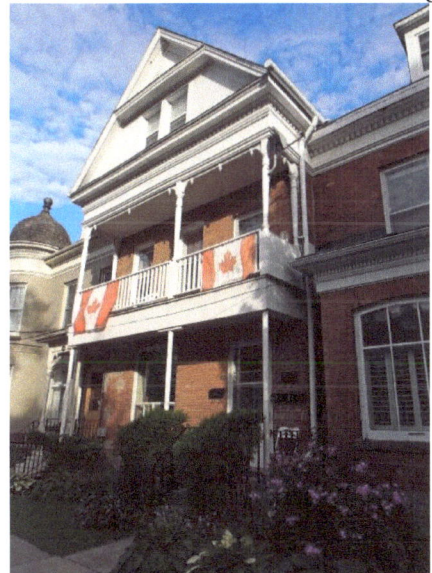

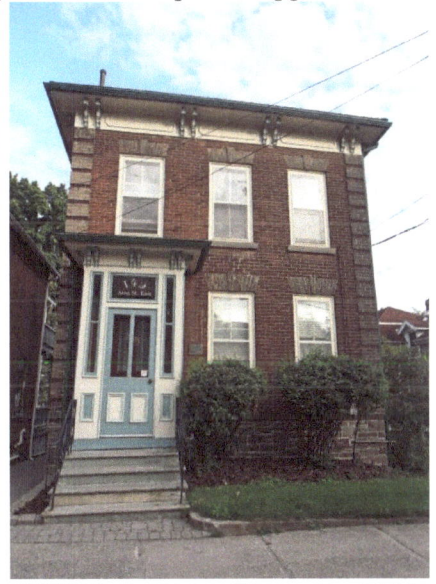

133 King Street West
Sunburst pattern in gable
2nd floor balcony with ornate
capitals

149 King Street East – c. 1880
David Simpson House
paired cornice brackets, corner
quoins, voussoirs with keystones

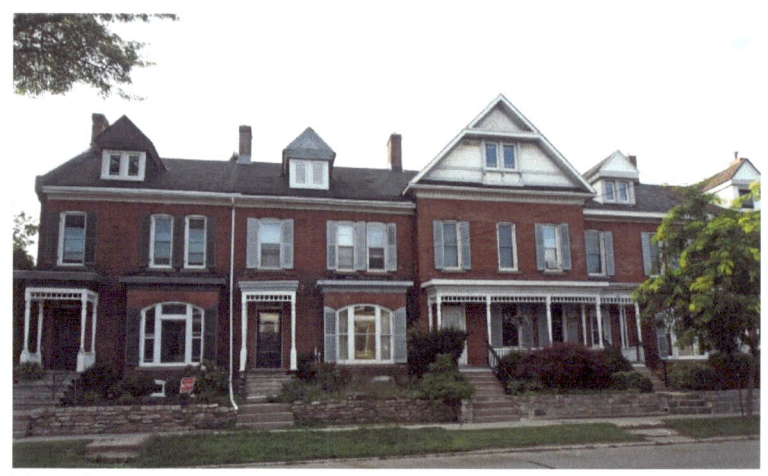

132-140 King Street East – St. Lawrence Terrace – built for William G. Tompkins – c. 1894 – wood turned columns for porches; dormers; central gable; rectangular bay windows

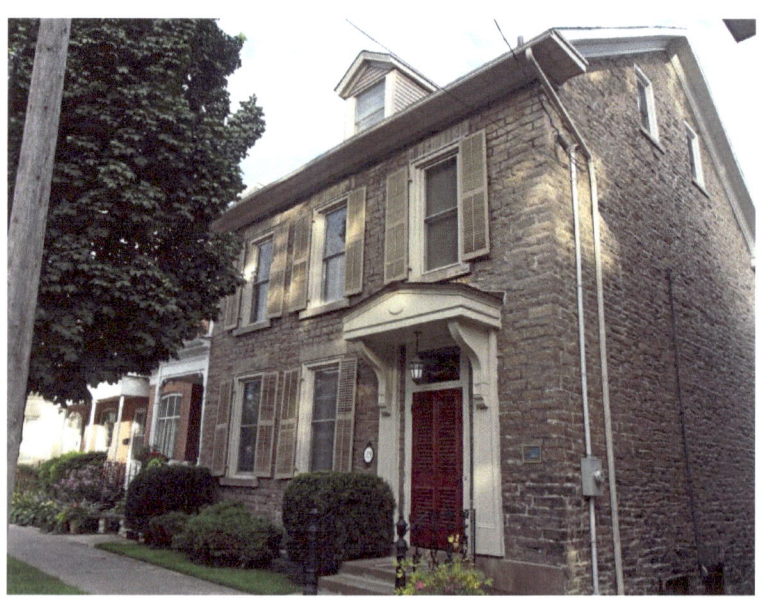

129 King Street East – Richard Bradfield House – c. 1852 - grey limestone, dormer

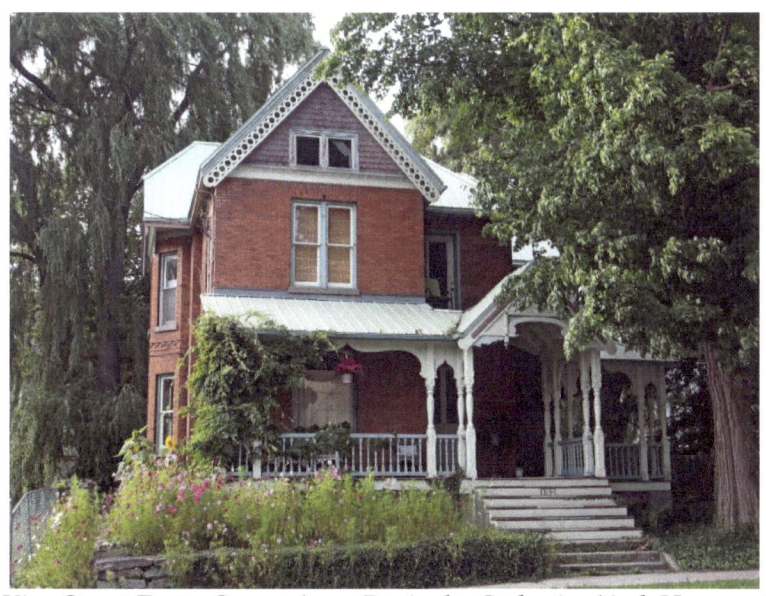

152 King Street East – Queen Anne Revival – Catherine York House – 1884 – gables with verge board trim, steep hip roof; ornate pillars with decorative capitals on verandah

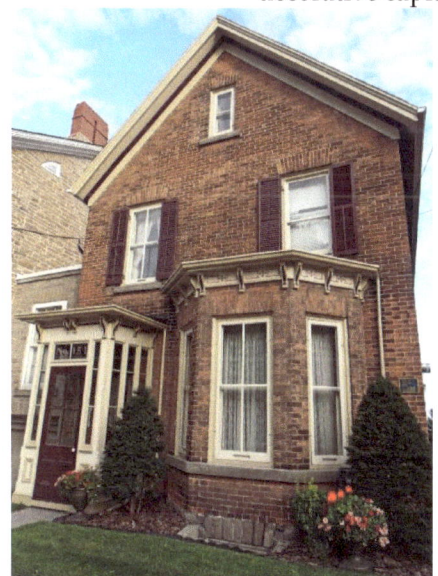

151 King Street East Henry and Ellen Soper House c. 1876 – frame building, bay window

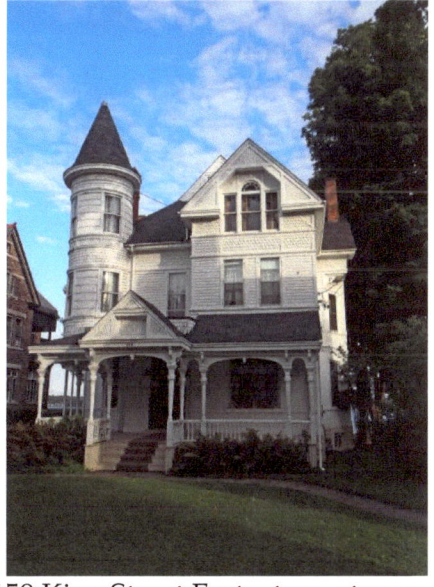

159 King Street East – two- storeys turret; frontispiece with gable, sunburst pattern, matching pediment above door

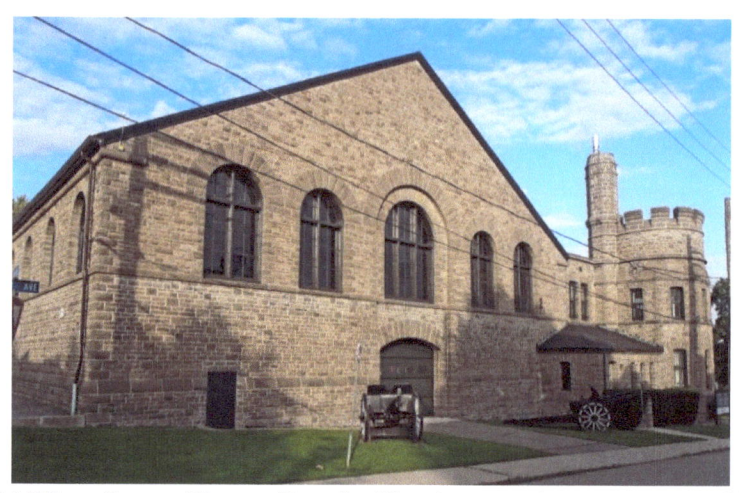

144 King Street East – Brockville Armouries – stone - 1900

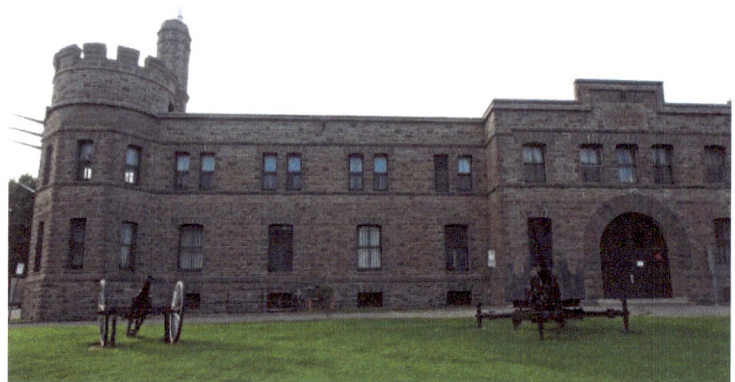

Romanesque style – battlement parapet, stone string courses

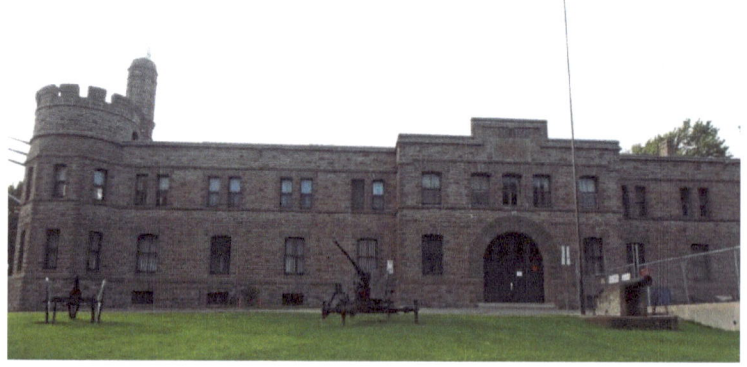

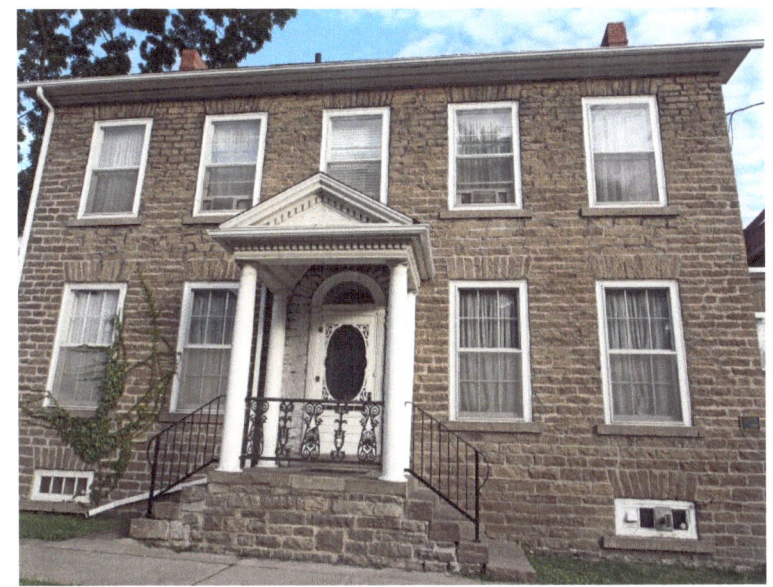

155 King Street East - Bartholomew and Ruth Ann Carley House – c. 1830 – pediment, dentil molding

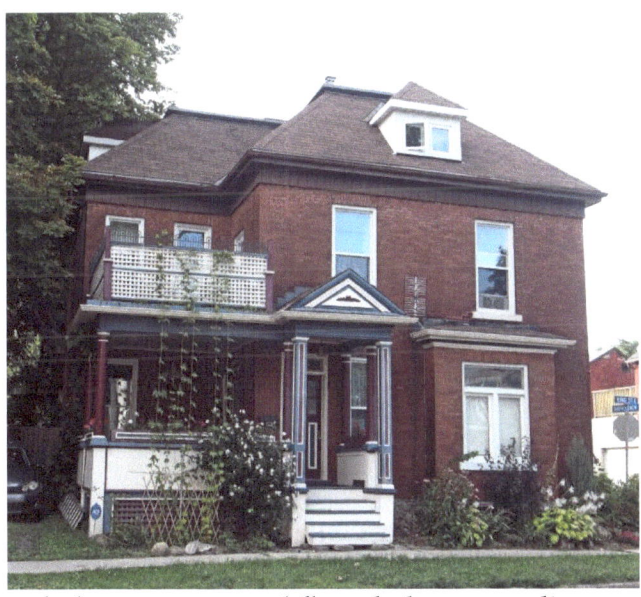

Hip roof, dormers, second floor balcony, pediment above verandah supported by rectangular and circular pillars, rectangular bay window

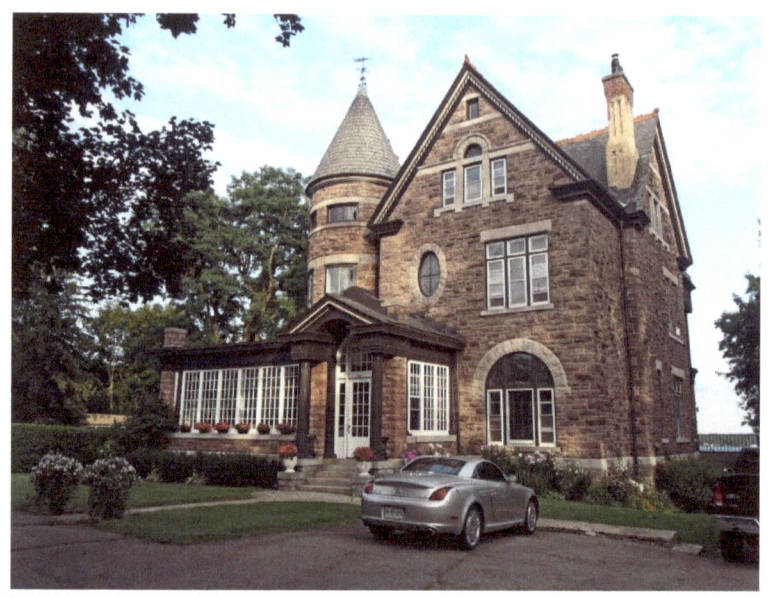

165 King Street East – Romanesque style, tower, Palladian window in gable with cornice return, large decorative chimney, round window arch, circular window, open pediment, enclosed veranda

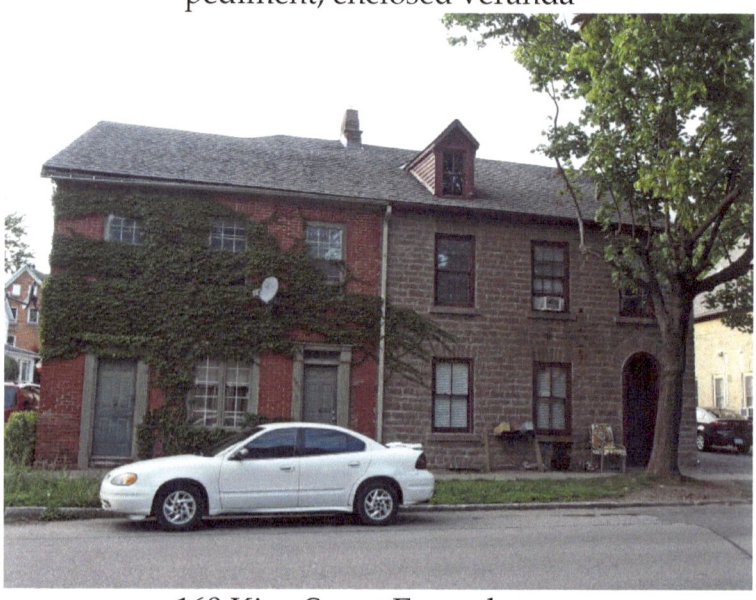

160 King Street East - dormer

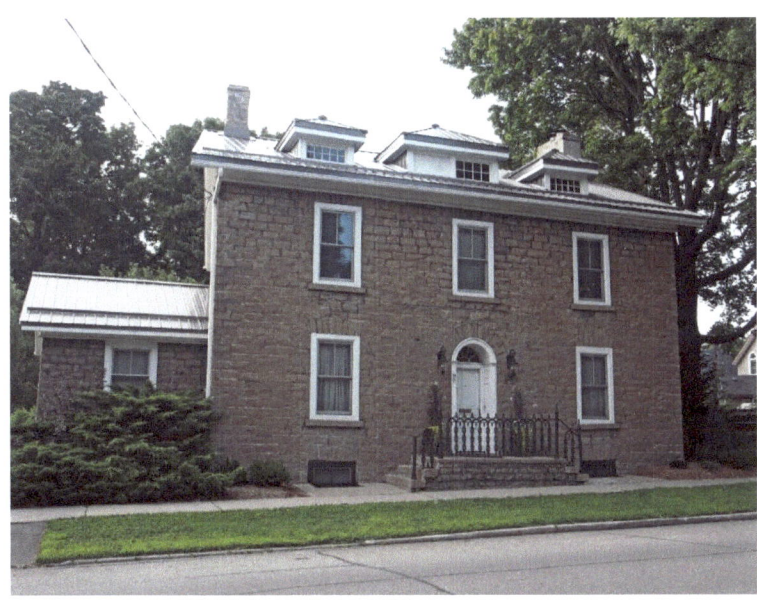

176 King Street East - dormers

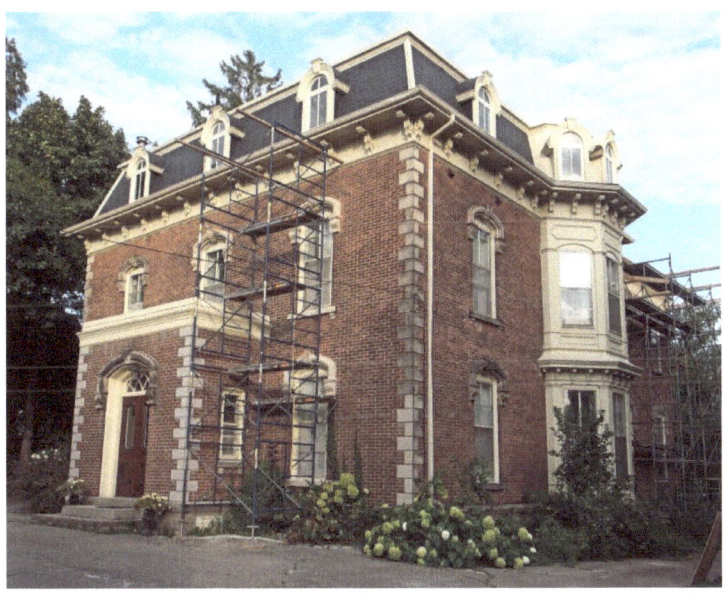

201 King Street East – Second Empire style – mansard roof
with dormers and window hoods, cornice brackets, decorative
lintels with keystones, corner quoins, two-storey bay window

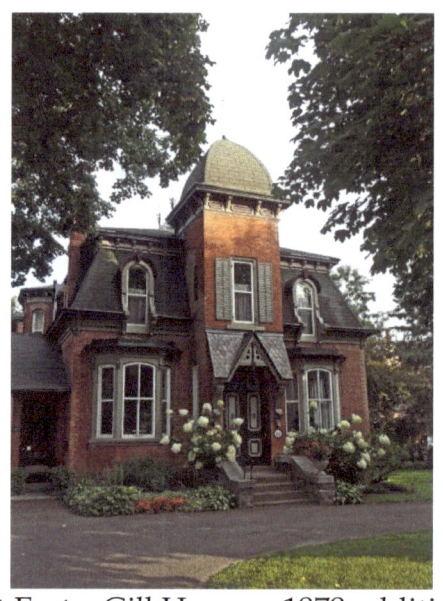

181 King Street East – Gill House – 1878 additions of roof and wings - Second Empire style, mansard roof, dormers, window hoods with keystones, iron cresting around rooftop balcony, central tower, bay windows

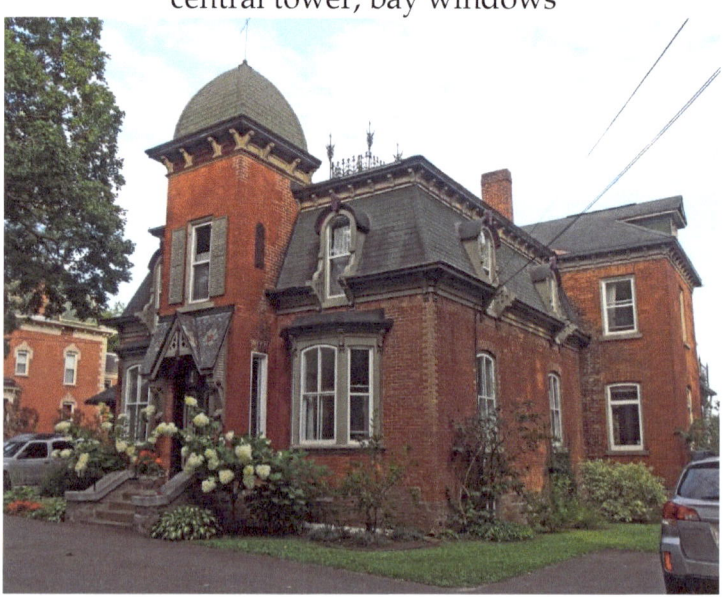

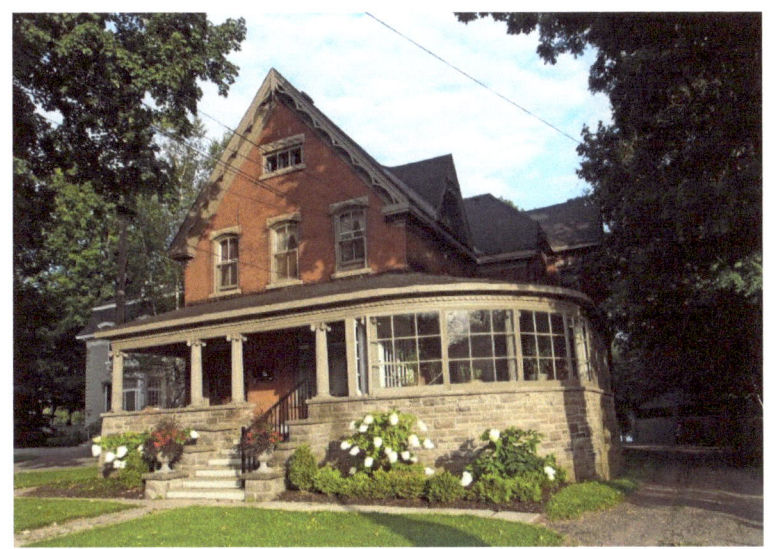

King Street East – Indian Cliff – residence from 1884 to 1905 of
Major James M. Walsh, Superintendent of the Royal Canadian
Mounted Police – he developed a strong friendship with the
famous Sioux leader Sitting Bull and successfully kept peace -
Victorian – steep gable with cornice return and verge board trim;
heavy stone lintels; Ionic capitals supporting wraparound veranda

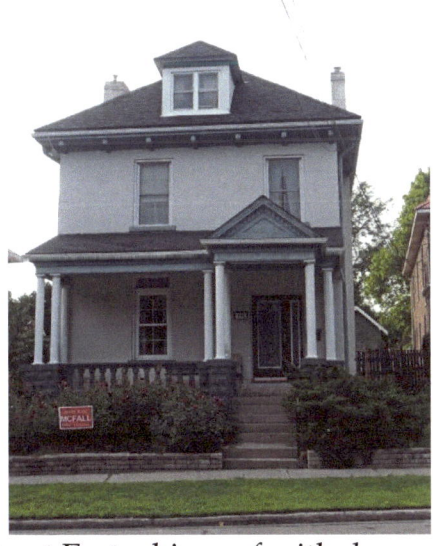

196 King Street East – hip roof with dormer, pediment

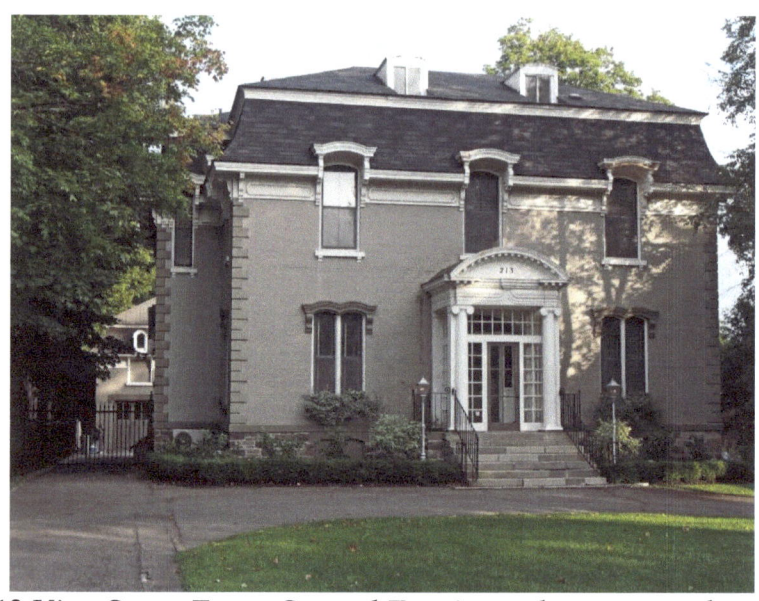

213 King Street East – Second Empire style – mansard roof, dormers, window hoods, ornate entrance with Ionic capitals, corner quoins

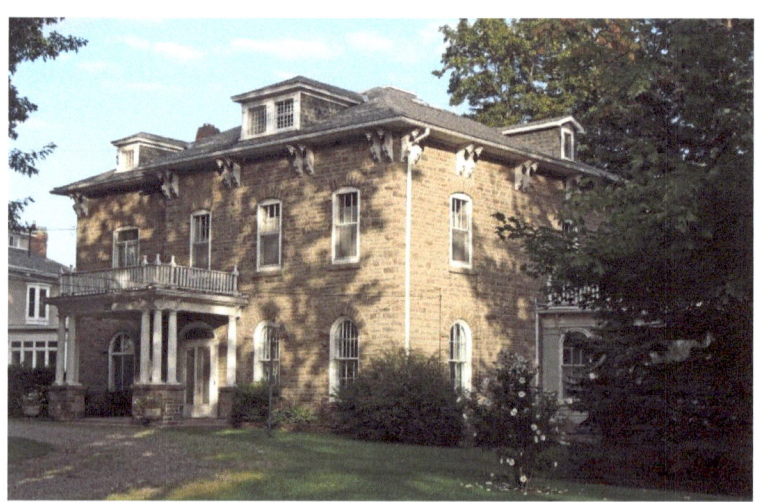

223 King Street East – William Jackson House – c. 1867 – Italianate - hip roof, dormers, wide eaves with paired cornice brackets, round-headed windows, a belvedere, verandas, balconies

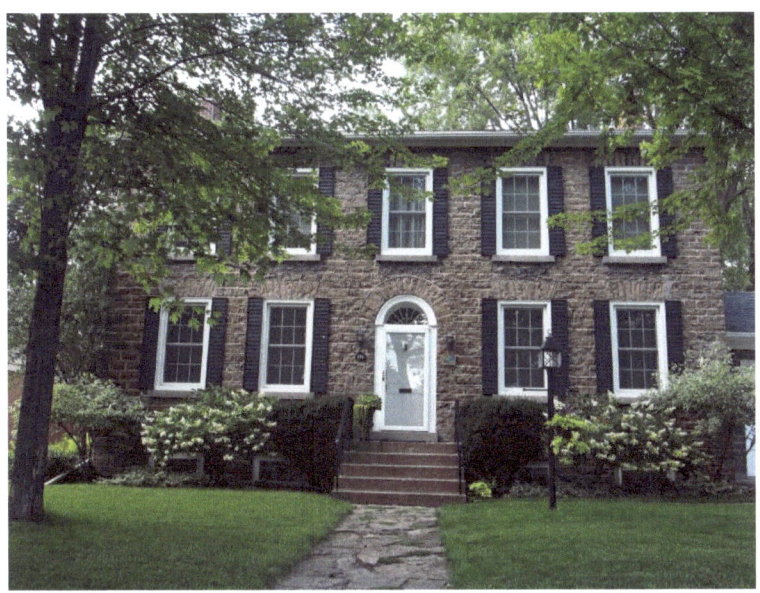

222 King Street East – Patrick Murray House - Neo-classical – stone, low pitch gable roof, quarter-circle windows, multi-light transom

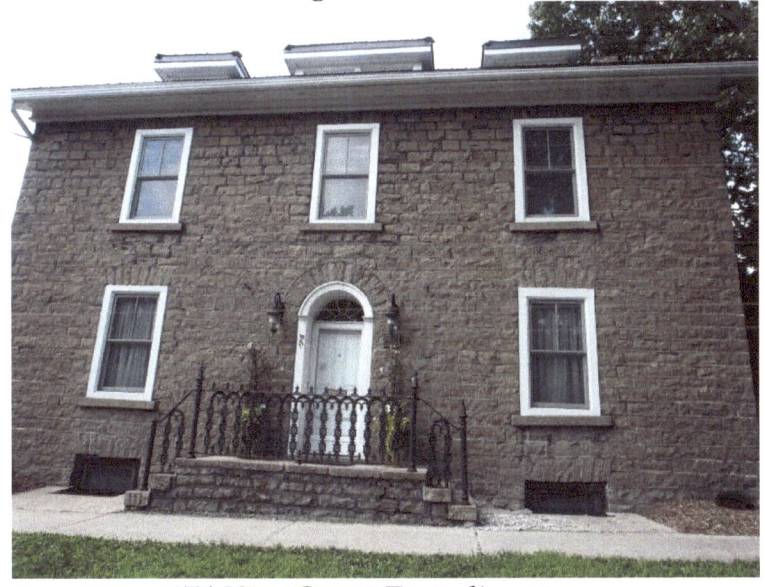

176 King Street East - limestone

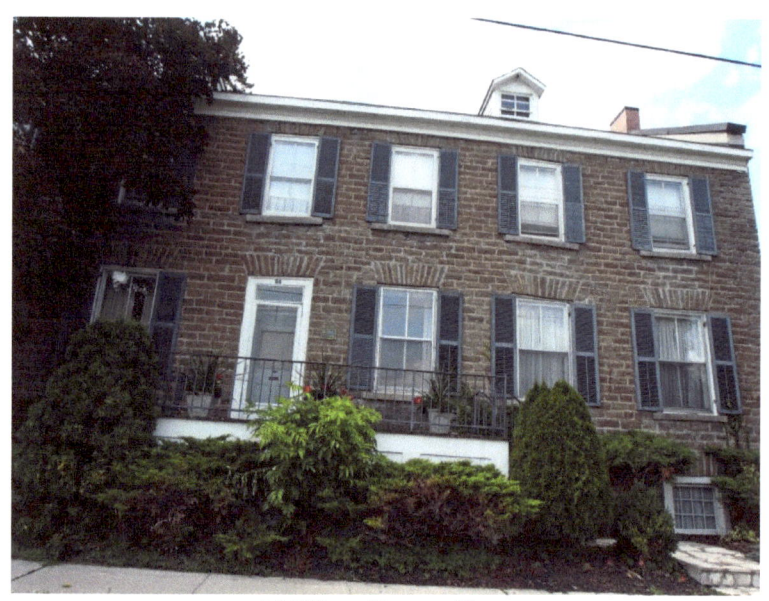

64 King Street East

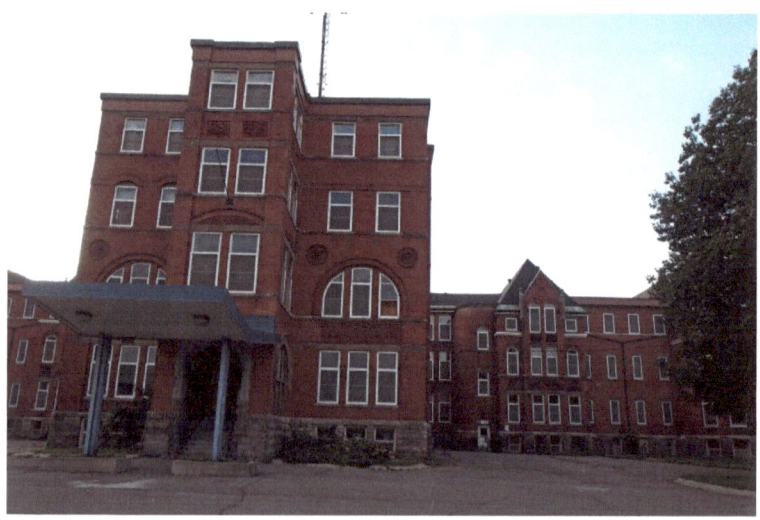

Old Brockville General Hospital – terra cotta patterning in brickwork, four-storey square frontispiece, semi-circular arches over triple windows on second storey; gabled frontispiece on three-storey section

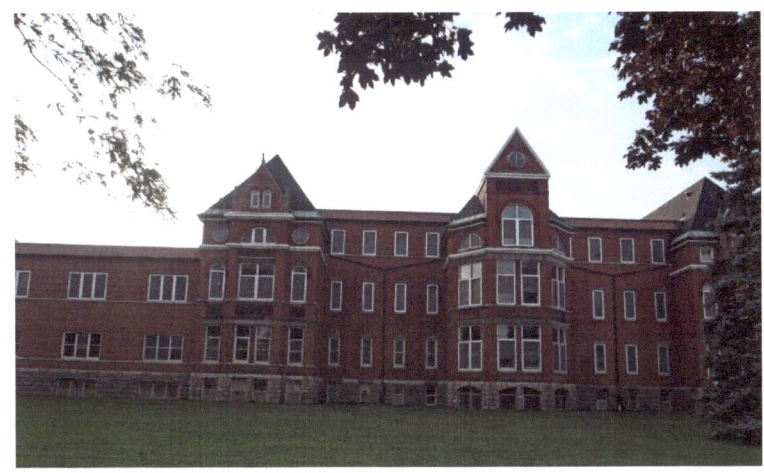

Old Brockville General Hospital, Elmgrove site (now closed) –
decorative gables, varied window shapes

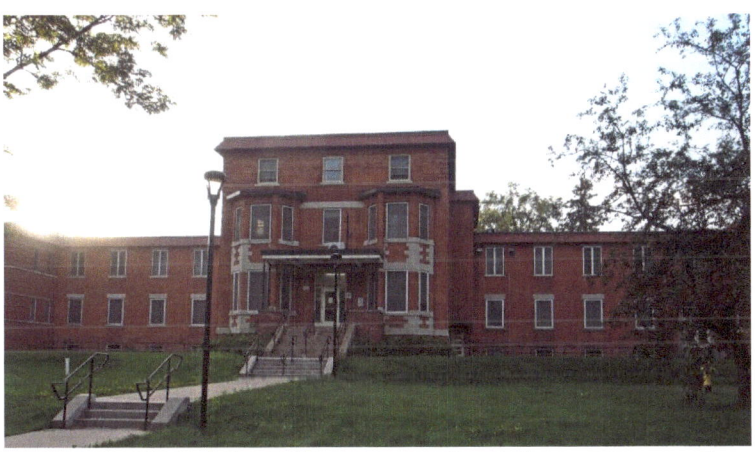

Dichromatic brick and stone work with two-storey bay
windows

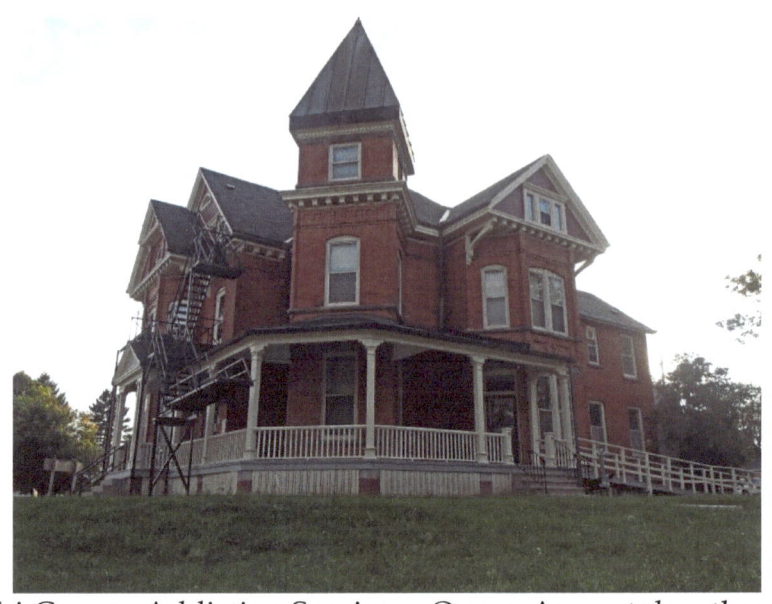

Tri-County Addiction Services - Queen Anne style – three-storey tower, gables, stone courses, open verandah with ornate pillars, open railing

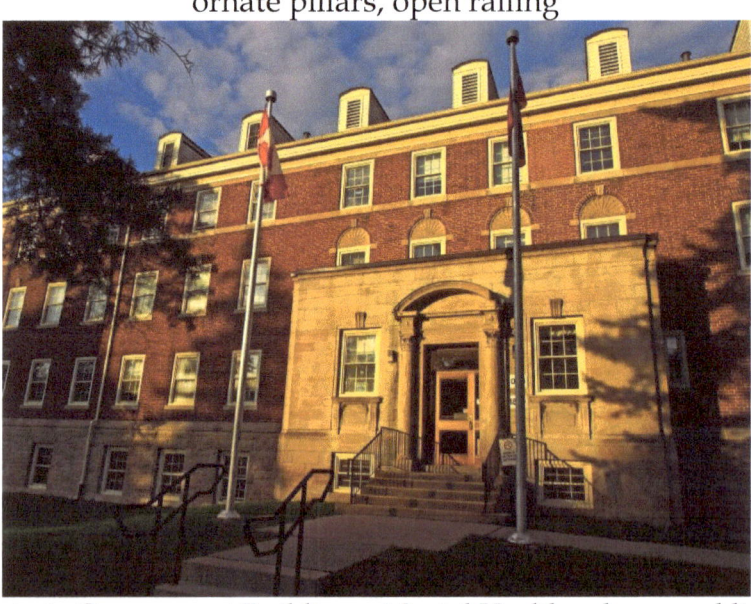

Ontario Government Building – Mental Health – dormers, blind transoms with voussoirs and keystones above frontispiece with engaged Corinthian columns and semi-circular open pediment

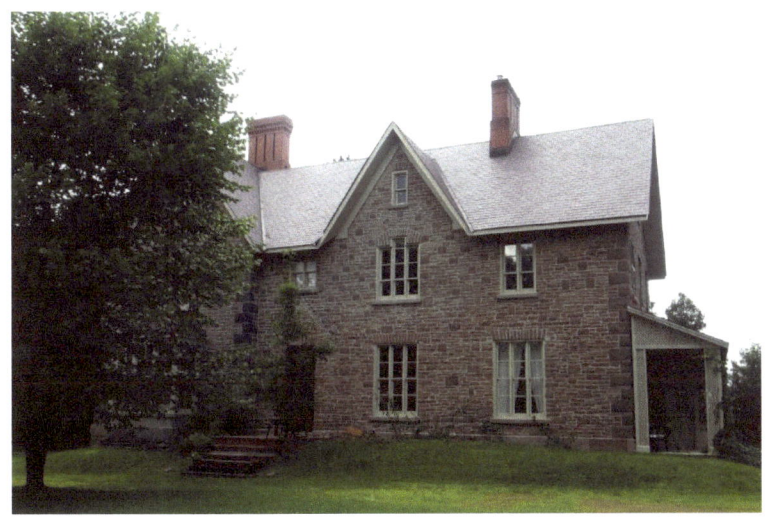

Gothic – large decorative chimneys, corner quoins, voussoirs

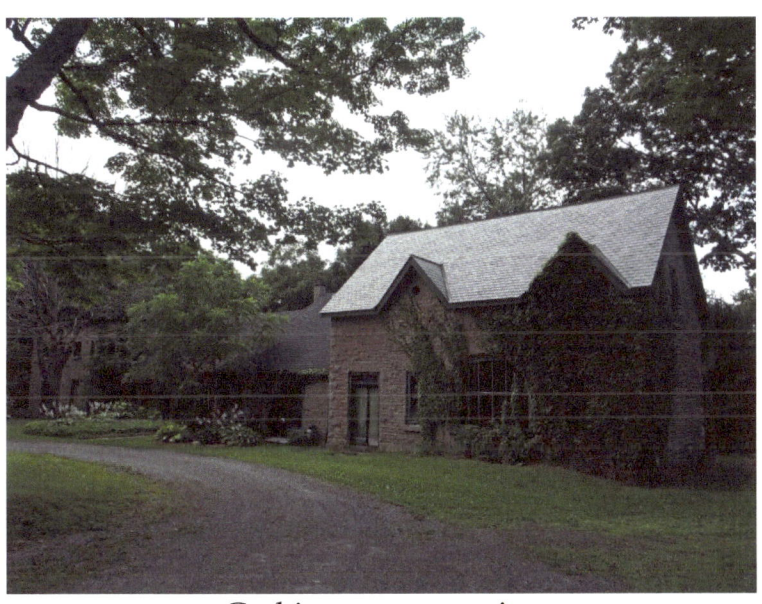

Gothic – corner quoins

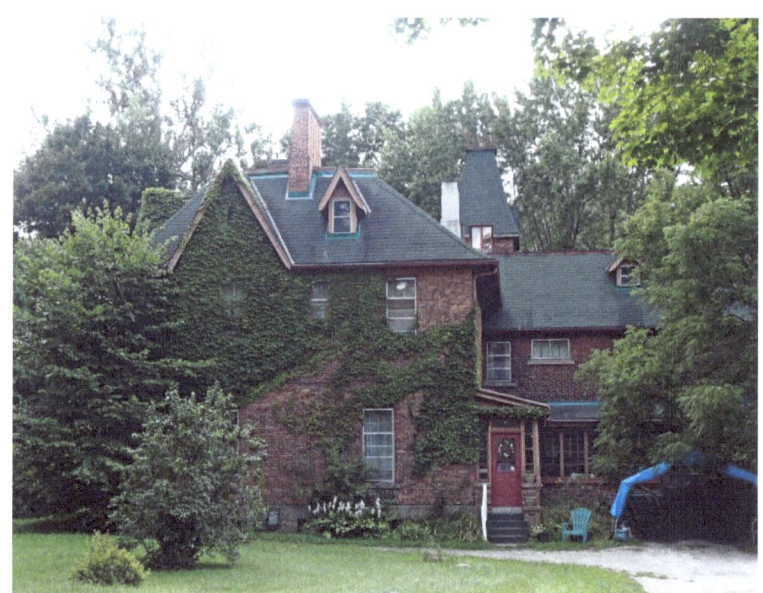

Queen Anne style – varied roofline, dormers, decorative
chimney, tower

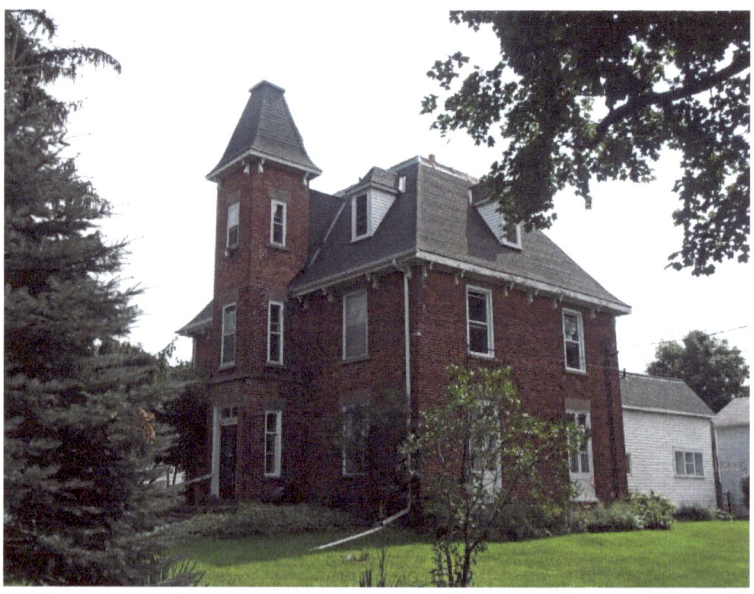

First Avenue - three-storey tower, dormers in roof, brackets

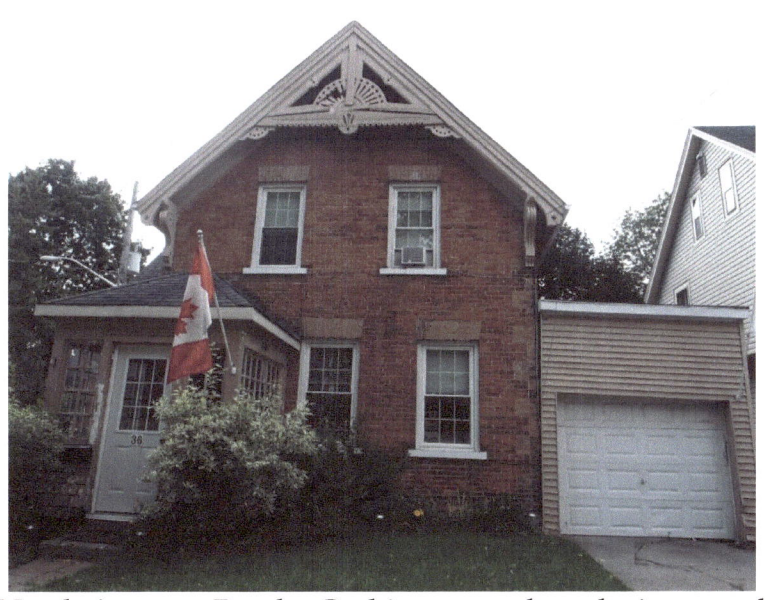

36 North Augusta Road – Gothic – verge board trim on gable, corner quoins

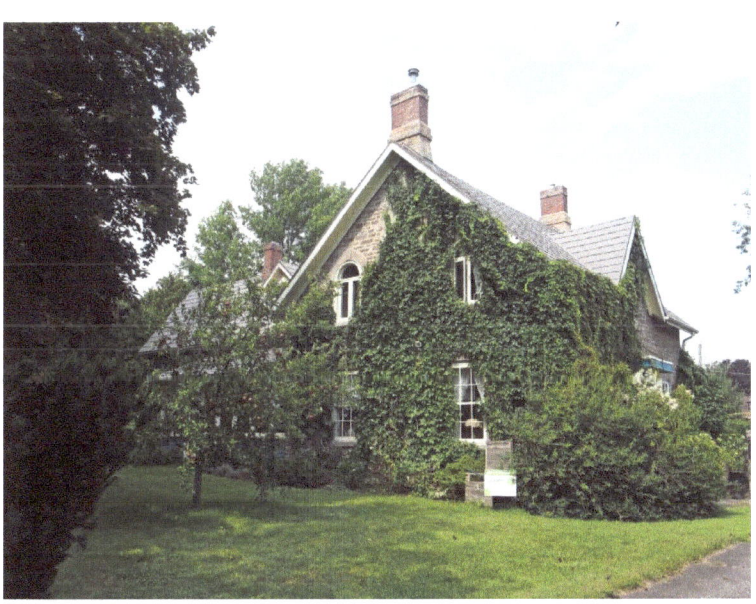

301 North Augusta Road – Sarah and John Lawrence House – stone and frame – 1860 – centre gable farm house

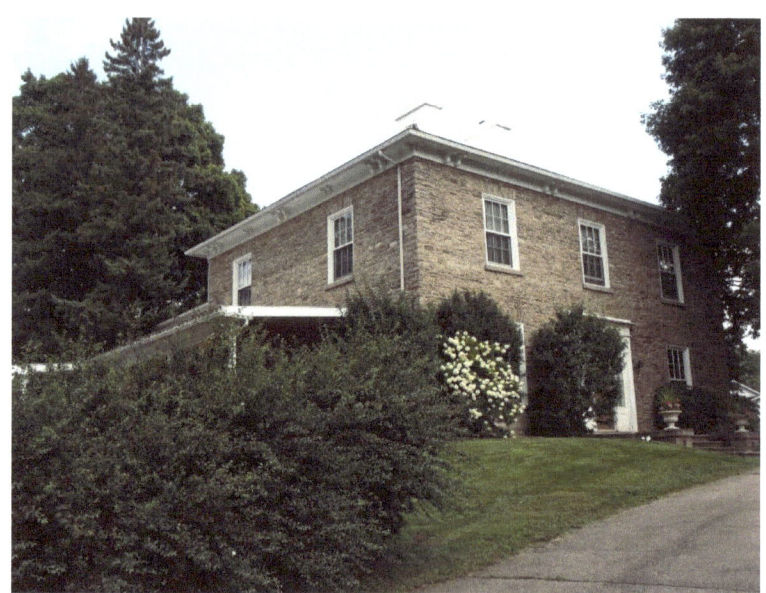

Cochrane Drive – Italianate – hip roof, paired cornice brackets

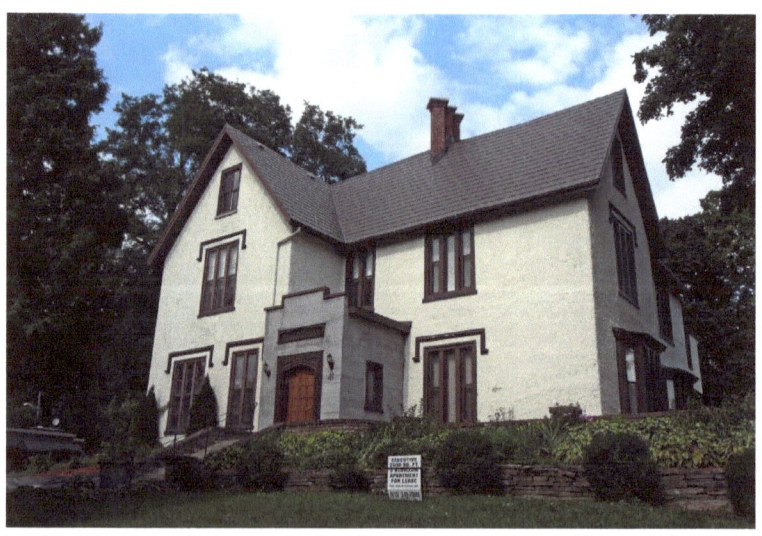

41 Cochrane Drive – Isabella and George Easton House
"Beauvoir" – 1853 – Tudor Revival

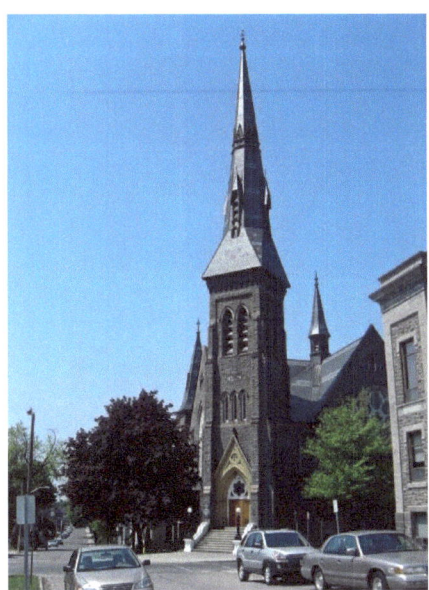
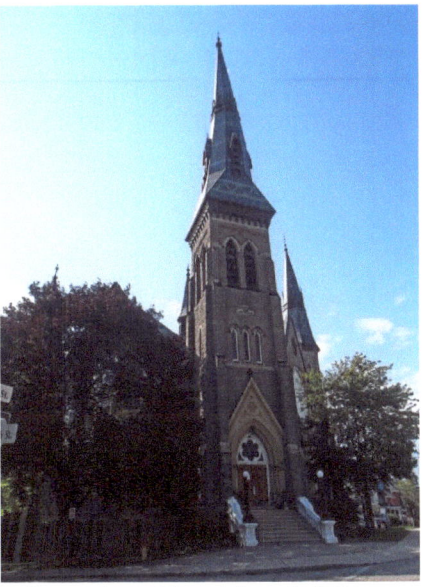

10 Church Street – First Presbyterian Church – 1879
Gothic Revival, lancet windows, buttresses, rose window, four
spires in a cross-shaped plan

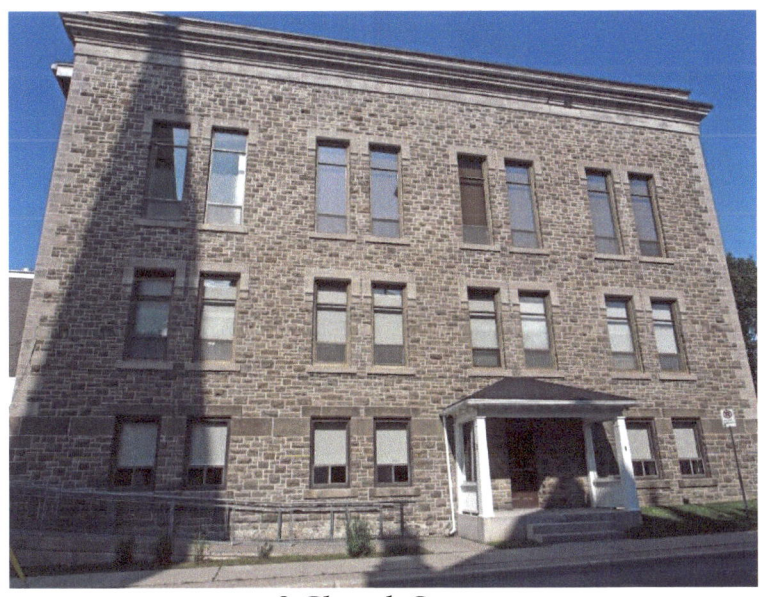

3 Church Street

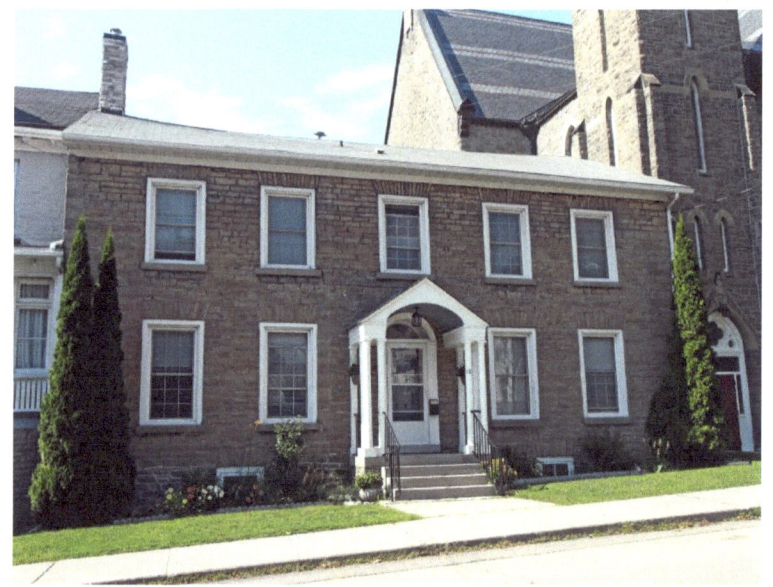

12 Church Street – Rev. William Smart House – c. 1820 –
Loyalist style stone building – balanced façade

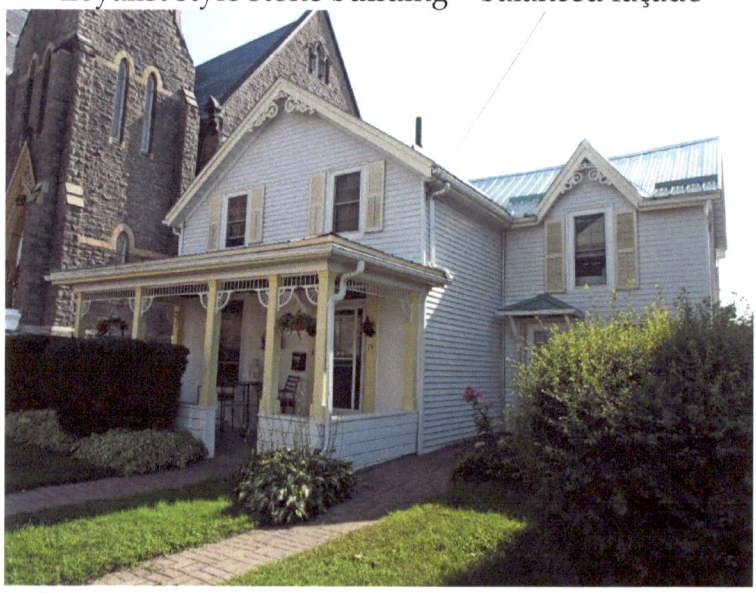

14 Church Street – Victorian – verge board trim on gables,
decorative porch trim at top of columns

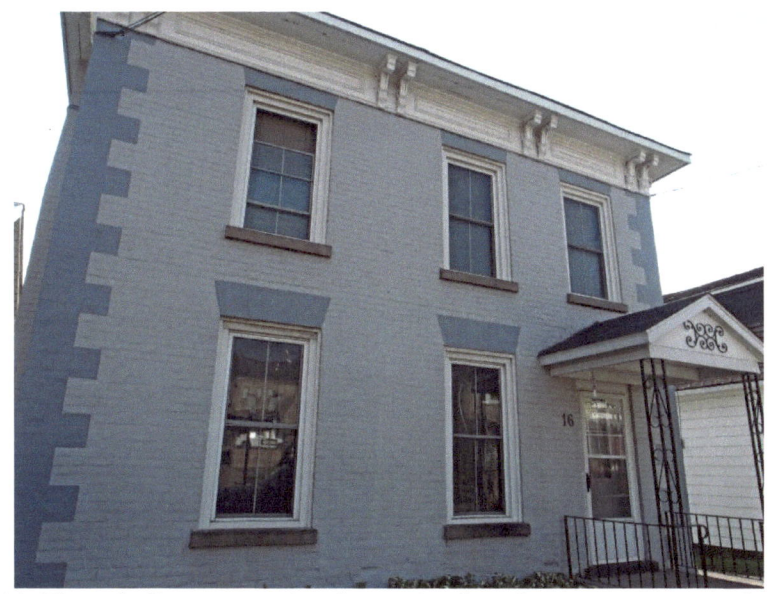

16 Church Street – paired cornice brackets, corner quoins

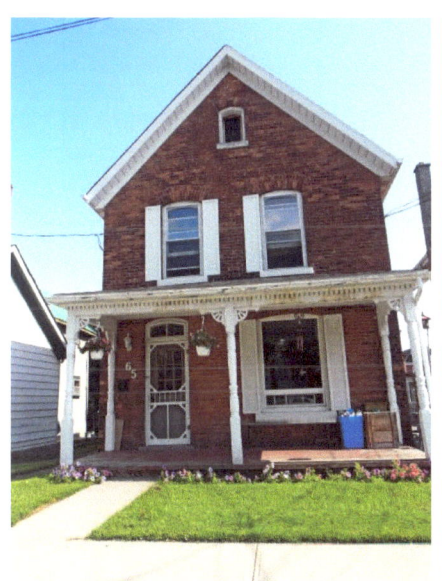

65 Church Street
Gothic

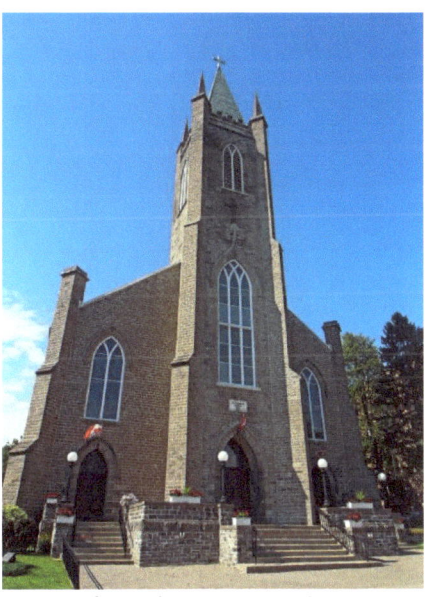

70 Church Street - 1856
Gothic - St. Francis Xavier
Roman Catholic Church

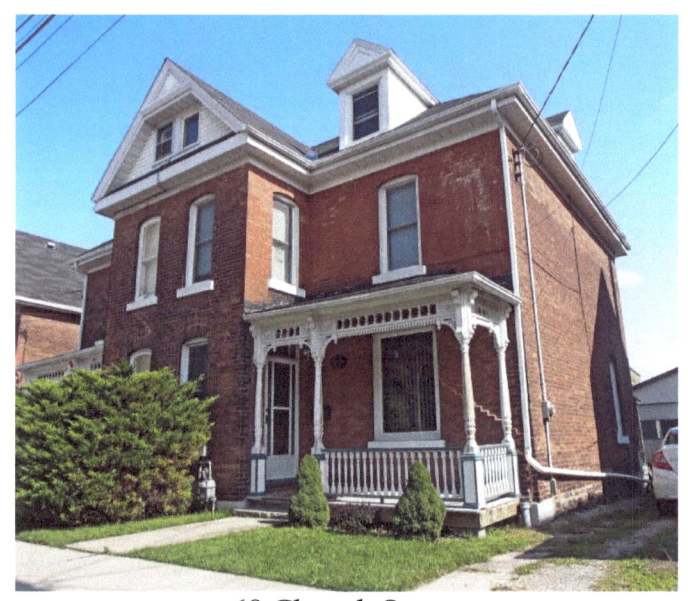

69 Church Street

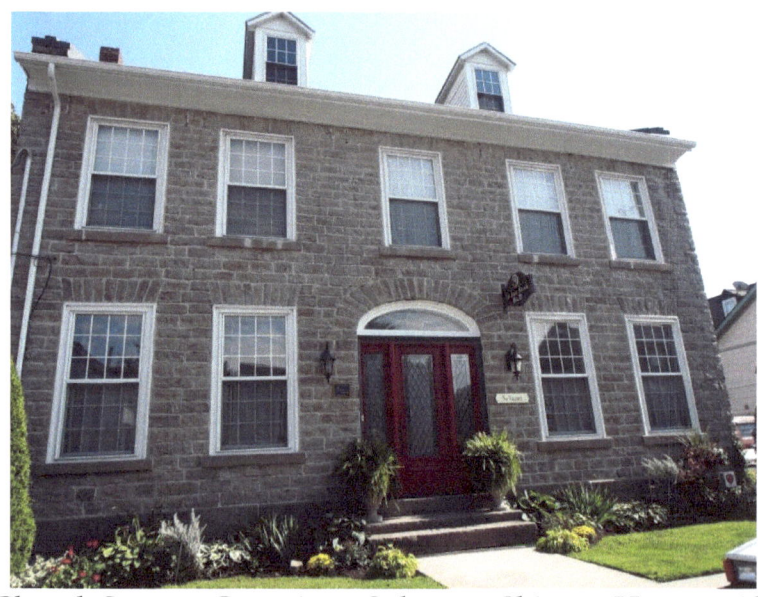

89 Church Street – Georgian - Sylvester Skinner House – 1830 -
Sir Isaac Brock Bed & Breakfast

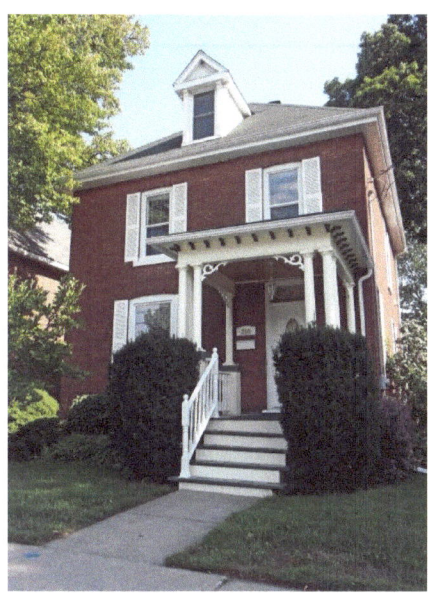

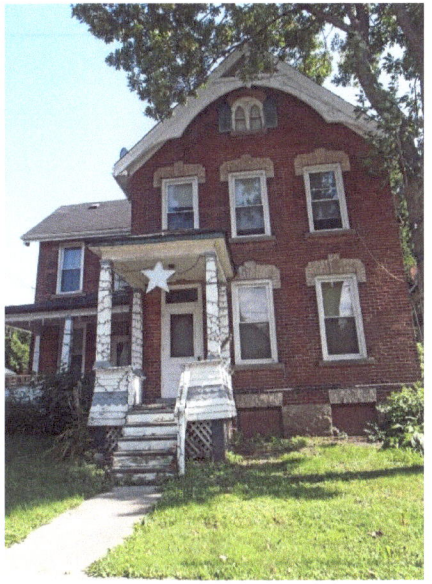

209 Church Street
Italianate, hip roof, dormer

Church Street
Gothic, verge board trim on
gable, lintels with keystones

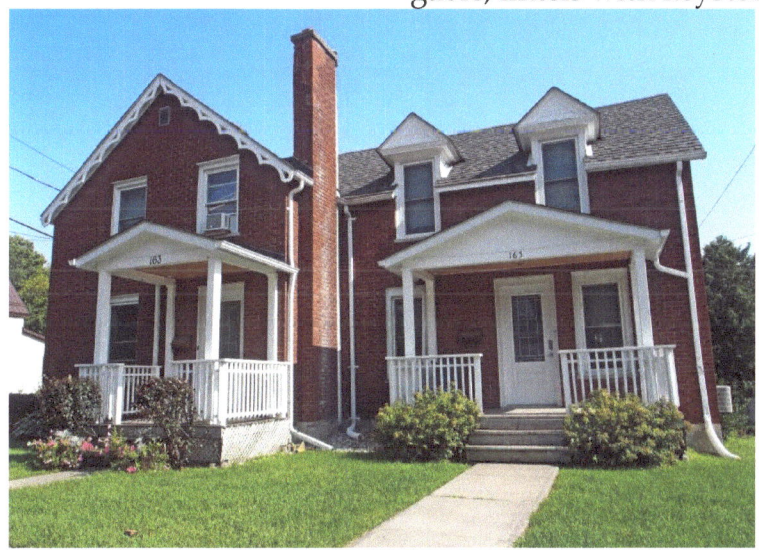

163-165 Church Street – verge board trim on gable, dormers,
pediments

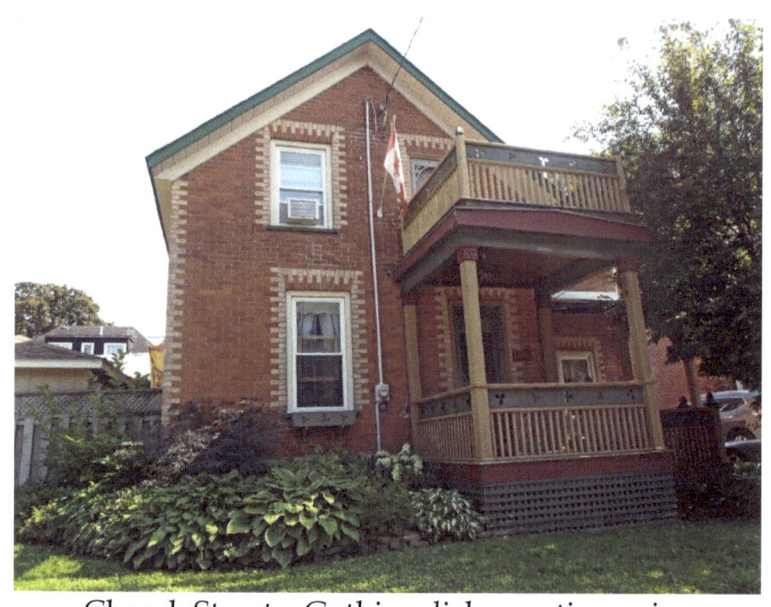

Church Street – Gothic - dichromatic quoins

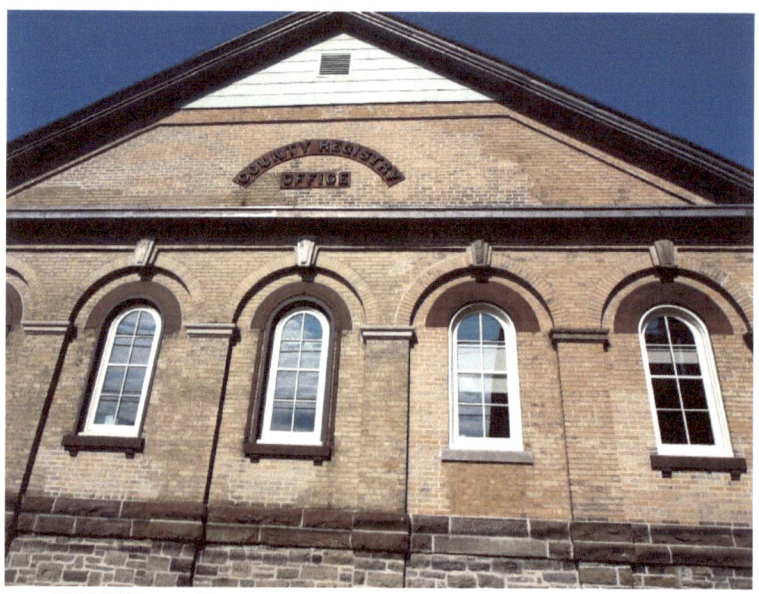

7 William Street - County Registry Office - 1872

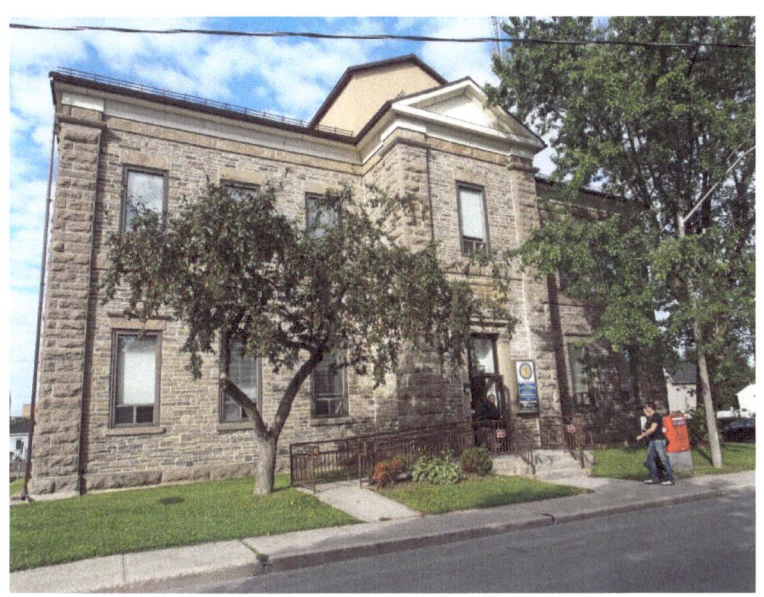

32 Wall Street – Victoria Common School – c. 1855 – frontispiece with pediment

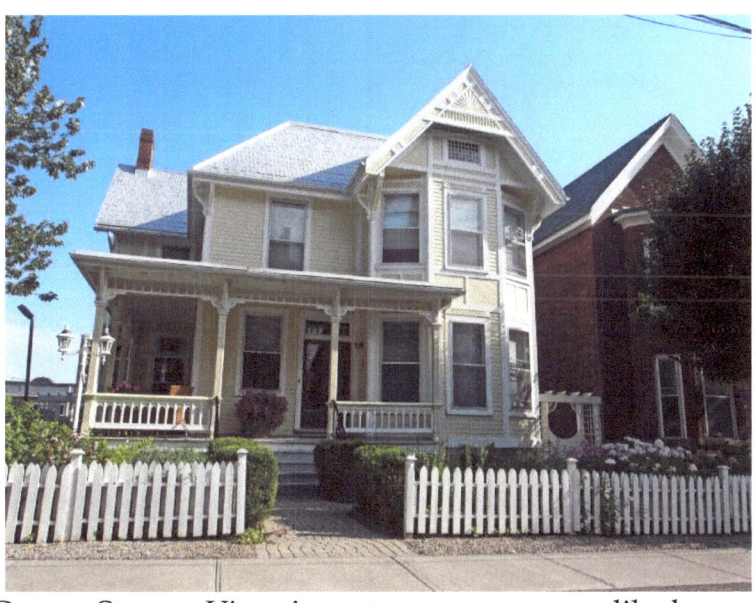

5 George Street – Victorian – two-storey tower-like bay with verge board trim on gable, decorative capitals on porch pillars

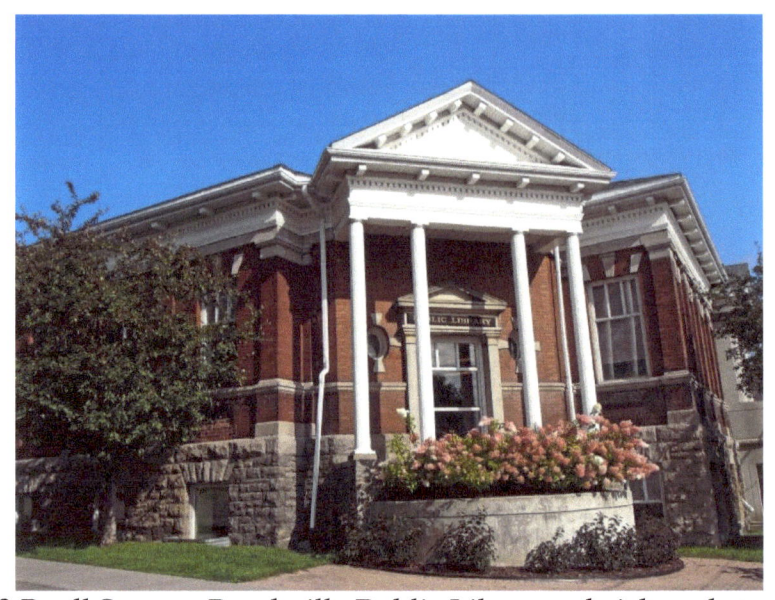

23 Buell Street – Brockville Public Library – brick and stone
Beaux Arts style

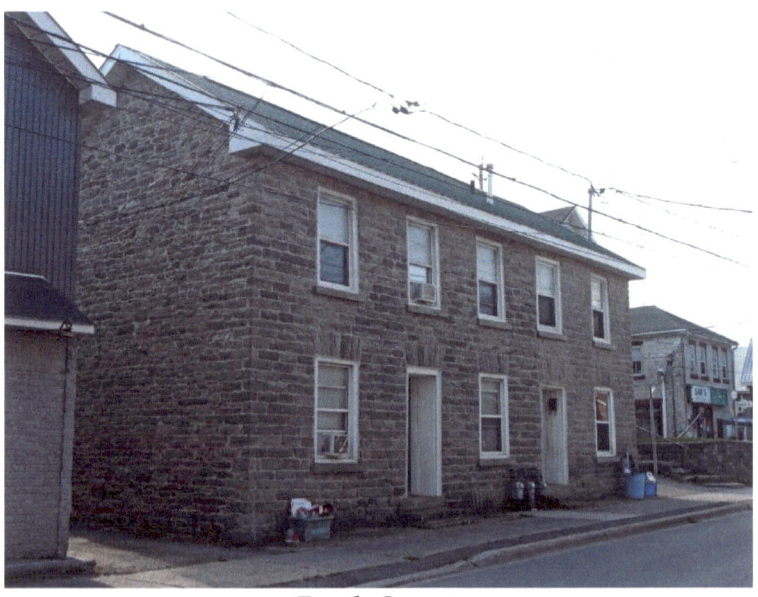

Perth Street

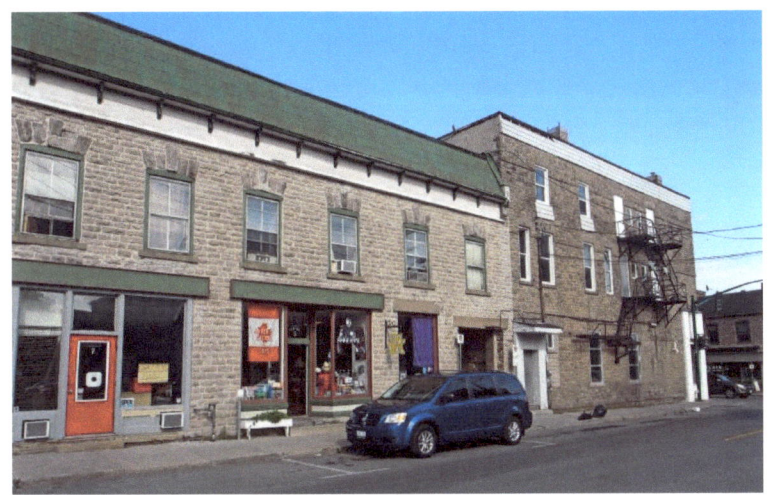

5-7 Perth Street

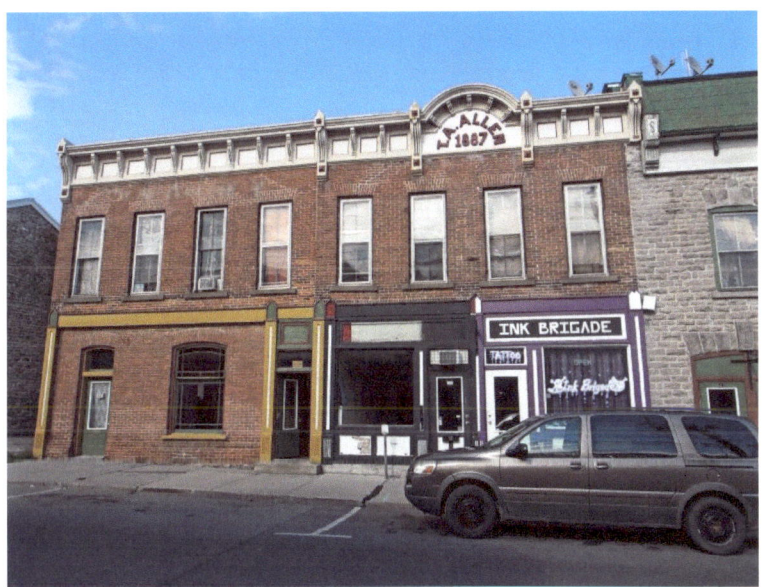

9-17 Perth Street – T. A. Allen Building – 1887 – cornice brackets

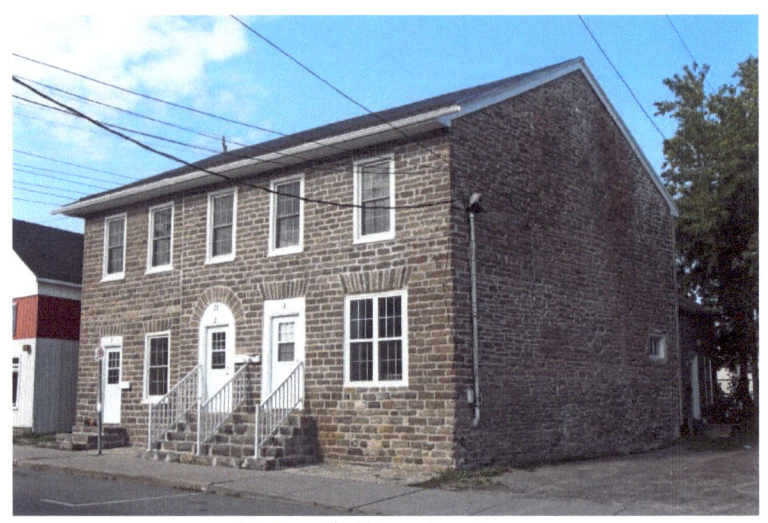

21 Perth Street - stone

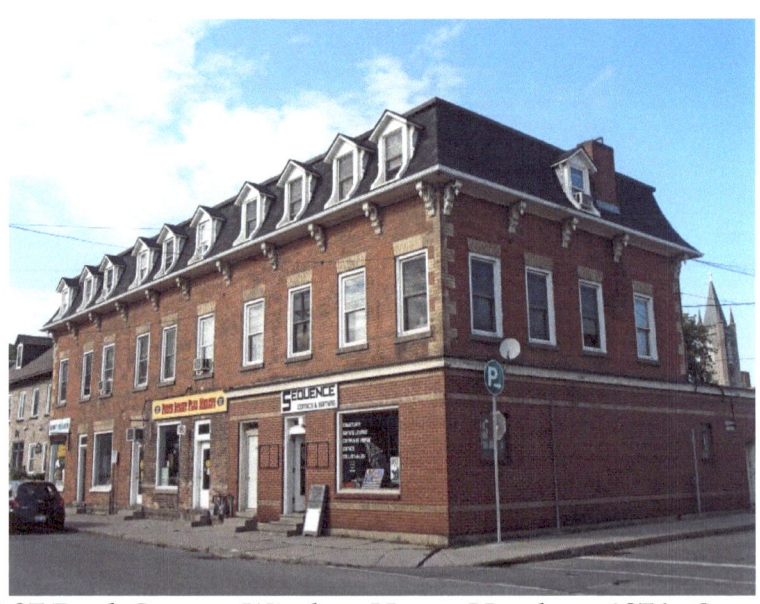

25-27 Perth Street – Windsor House Hotel – c. 1876 - Second
Empire style – mansard roof, dormers, cornice brackets,
dichromatic brickwork, corner quoins, banding

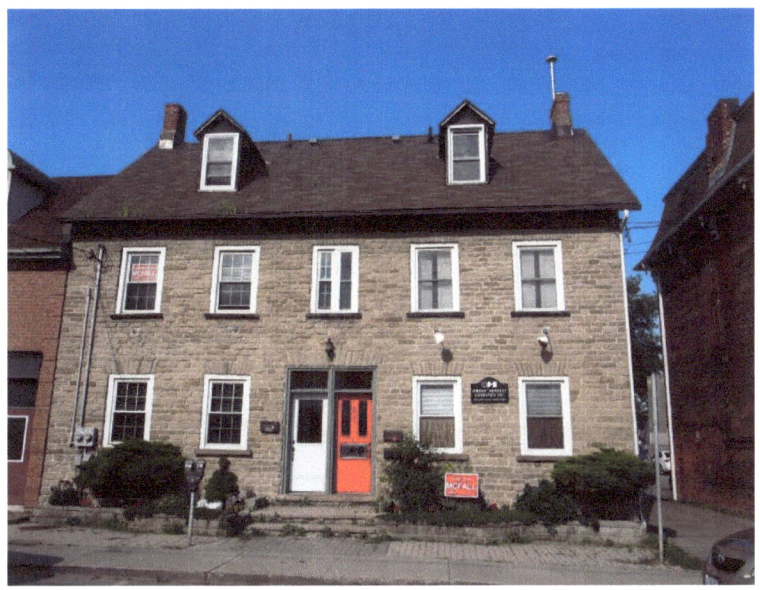

33-35 Perth Street – The Skinner House – c. 1824 - Georgian –
balanced façade, stone, steep pitched roof with dormers

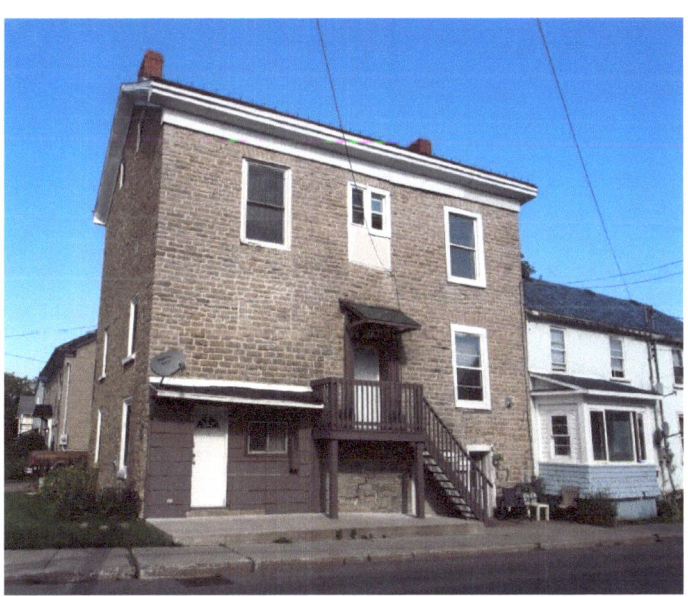

Perth Street – Elizabeth and James Hall House – 1820

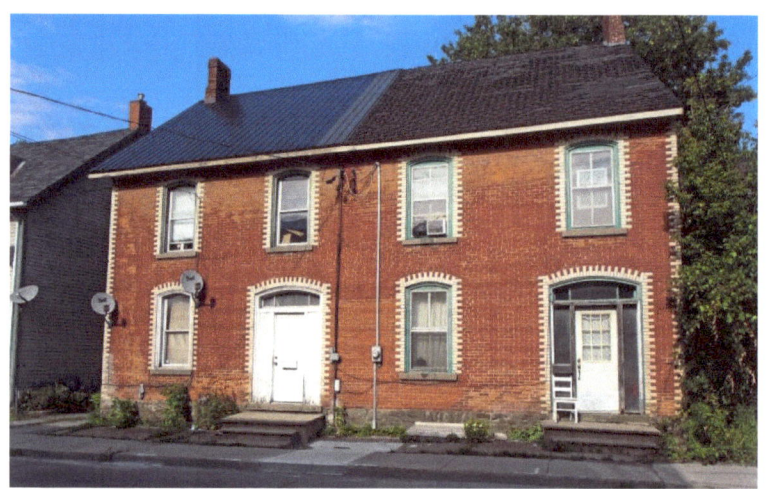

69-71 Perth Street – dichromatic brickwork

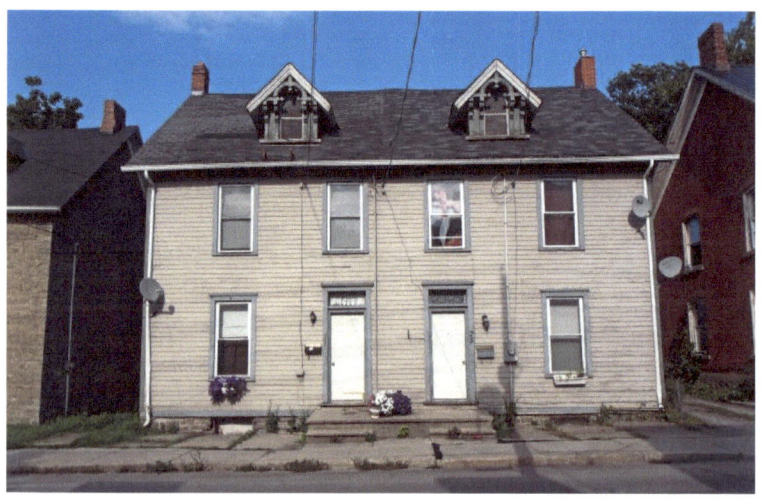

75-77 Perth Street – clapboard, dormers

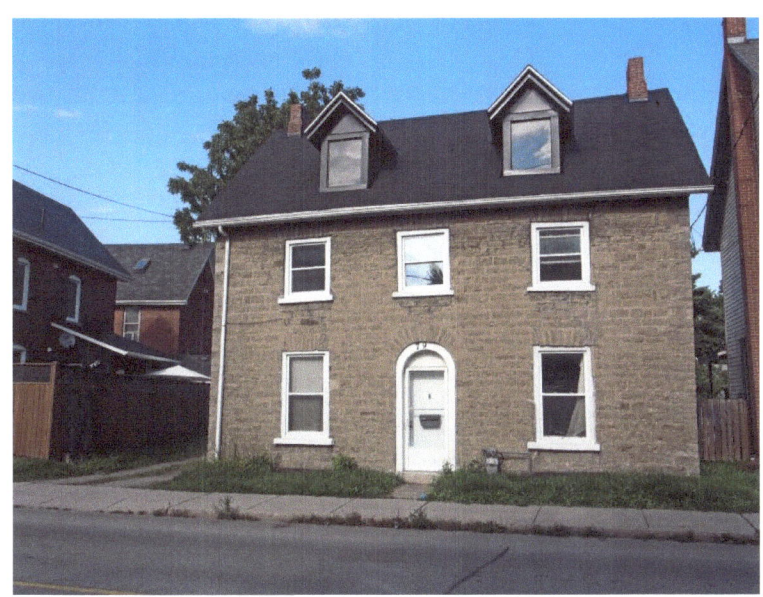

79 Perth Street - dormers

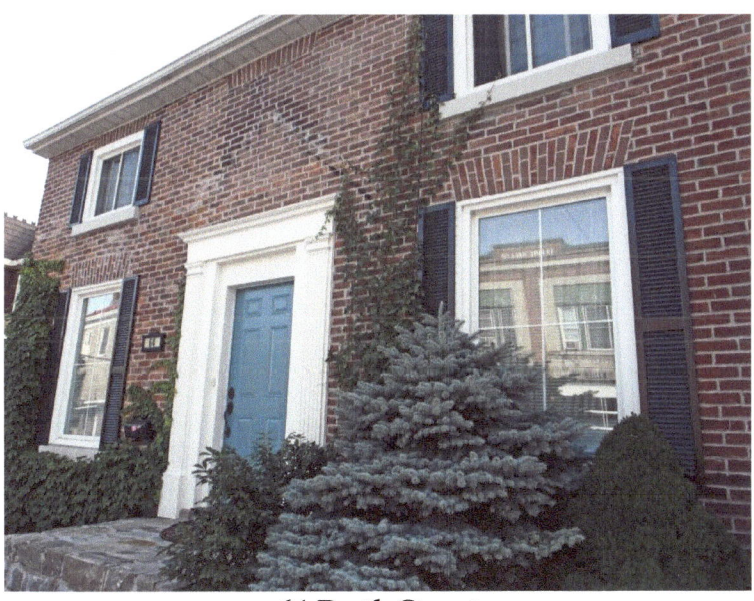

64 Perth Street

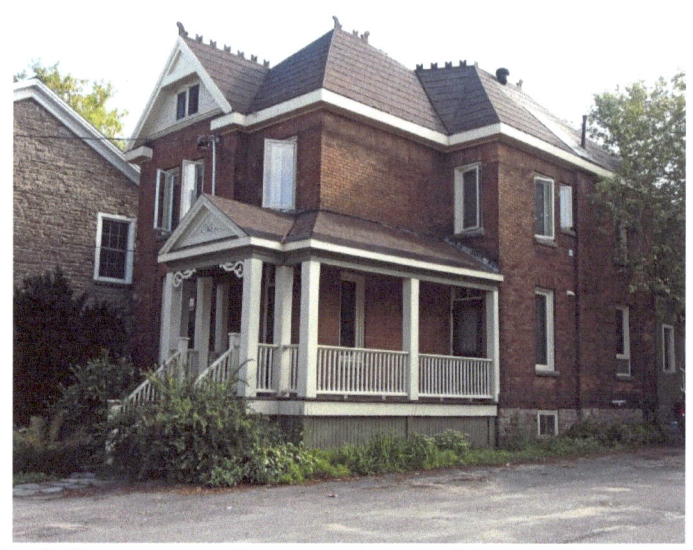

Perth Street – cornice return on gable, pediment with decorative tympanum, bric-a-brac on veranda, open railing

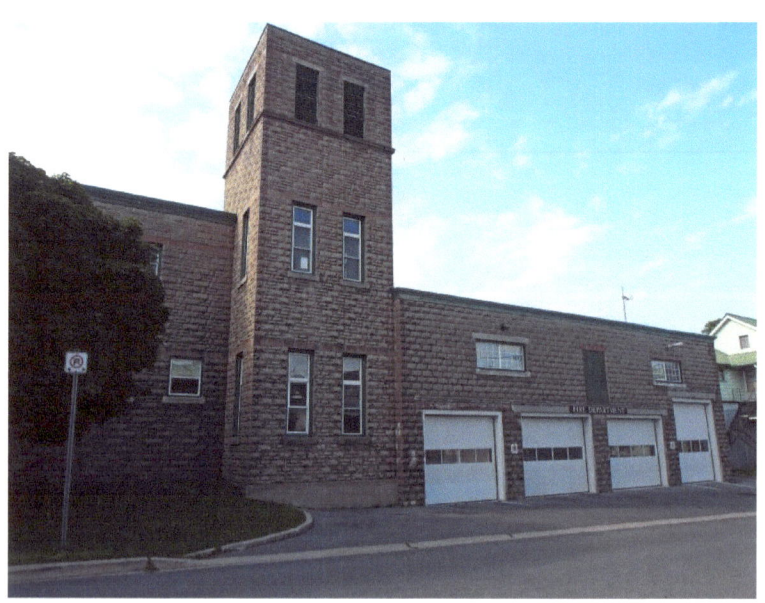

Perth Street – Fire Department

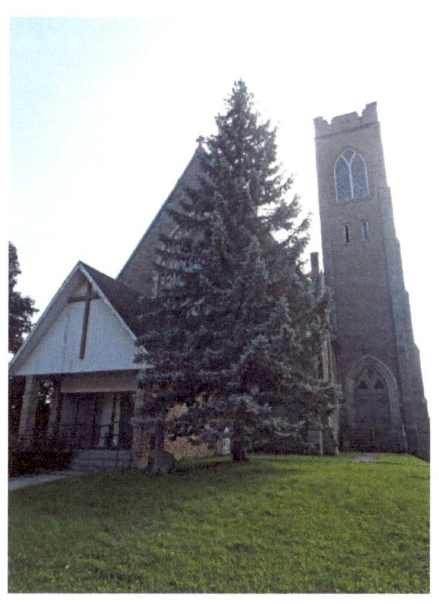

Clarissa Street – Trinity Anglican Church – 1877 – Gothic Revival - battlemented parapet on tower, lancet windows, polychromatic brickwork around large window, trefoils on tower door

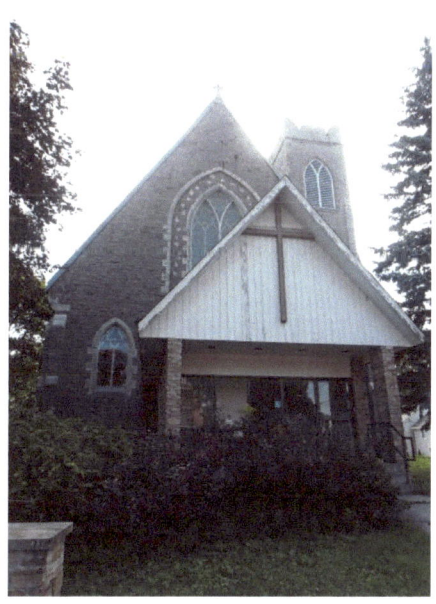

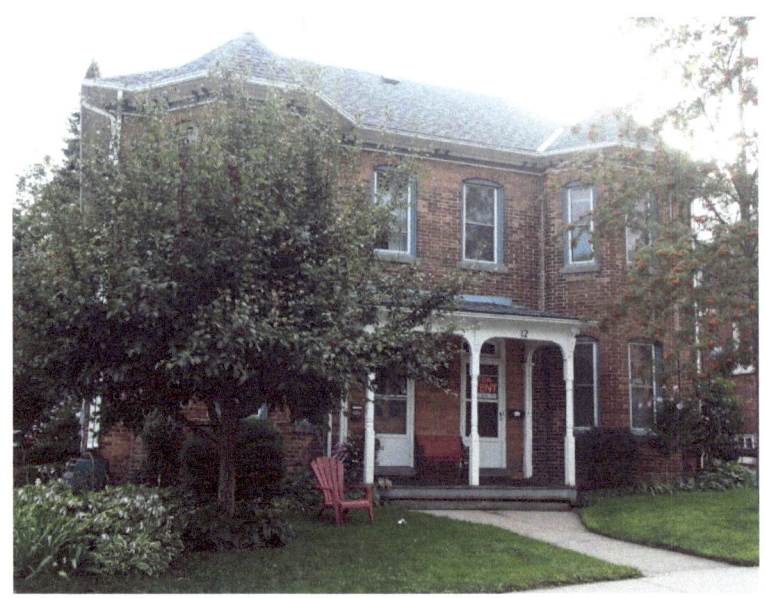

10-12 East Avenue – hip roof, two-storey tower-like bays

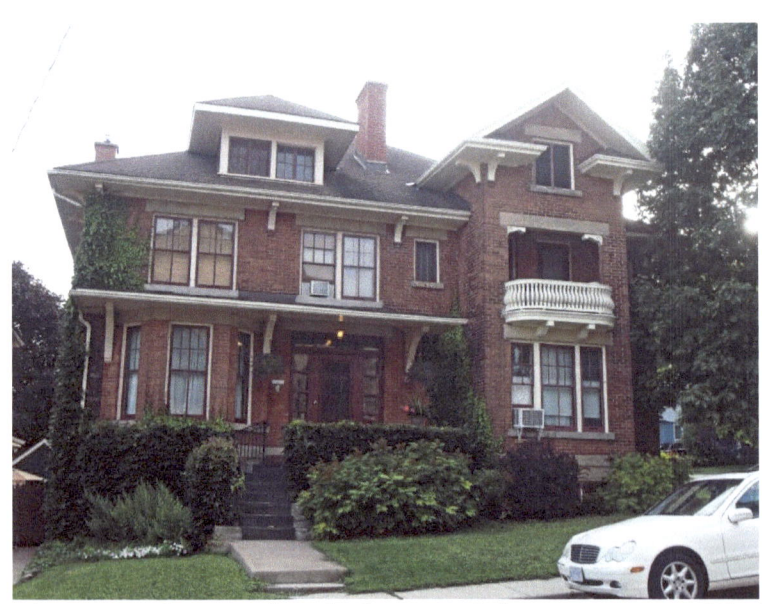

East Avenue – hip roof with dormer, 2½-storey tower-like bay
with second floor balcony, cornice return on gable, cornice
brackets, sidelights, transom

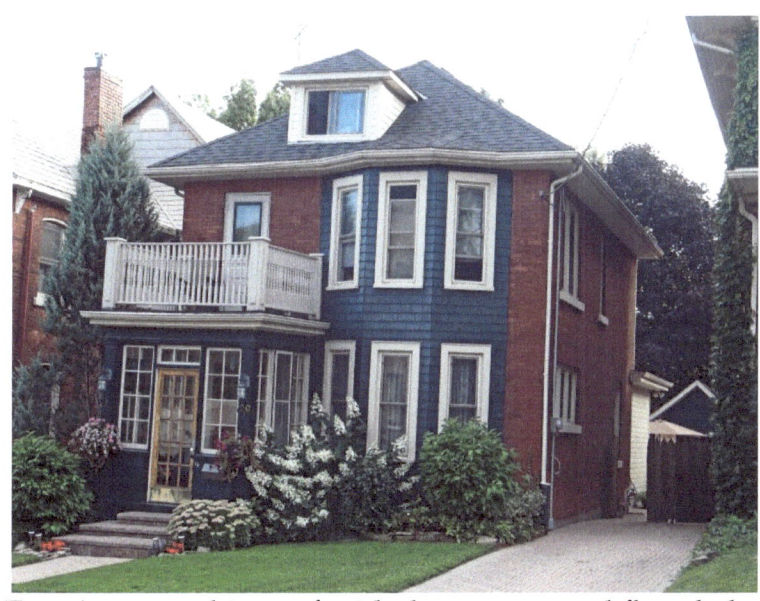

20 East Avenue – hip roof with dormer, second floor balcony above enclosed porch

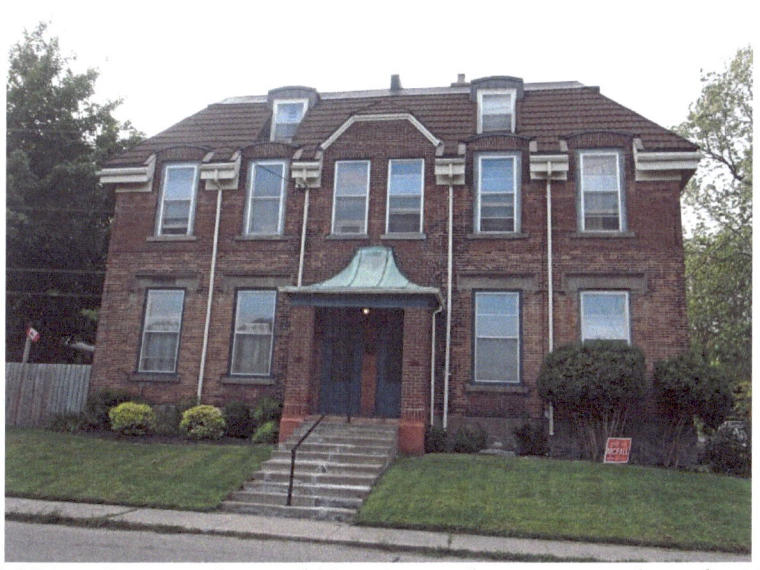

126 Pine Street – Second Empire style – mansard roof with dormers

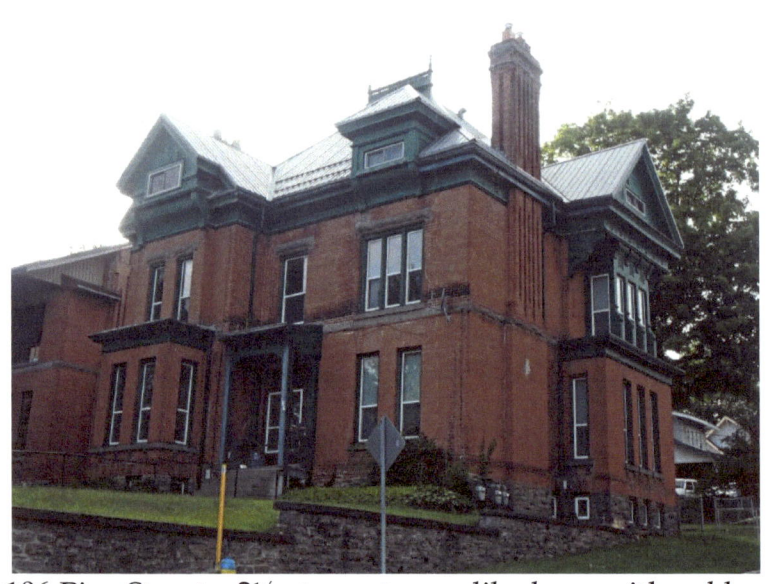

106 Pine Street – 2½-storey tower-like bays with gables, fretwork

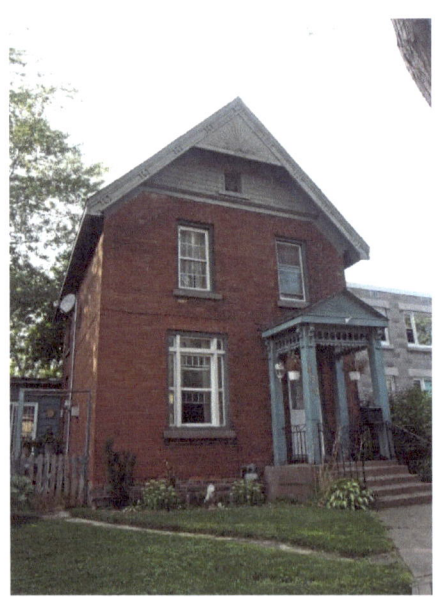

130 Pine Street – Gothic – verge board trim on gable, porch with decorative trim, pediment with sunburst pattern

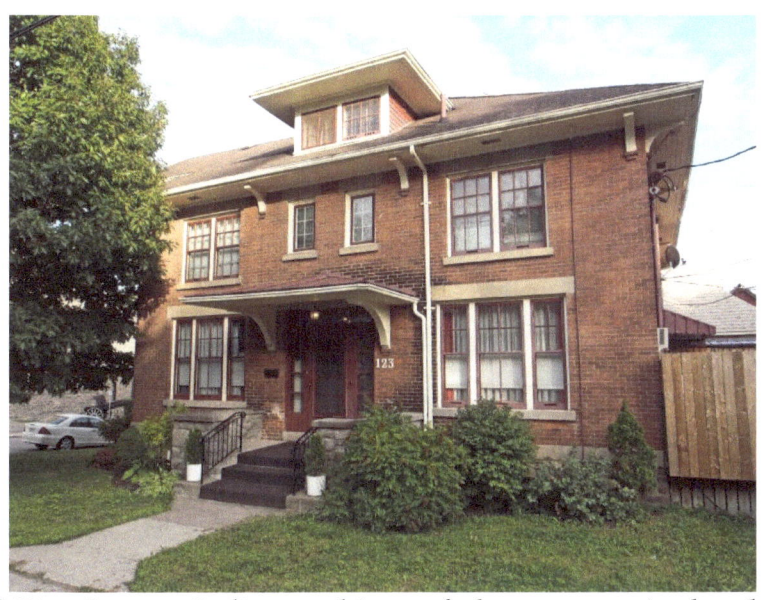

123 Pine Street – Italianate, hip roof, dormer, cornice brackets

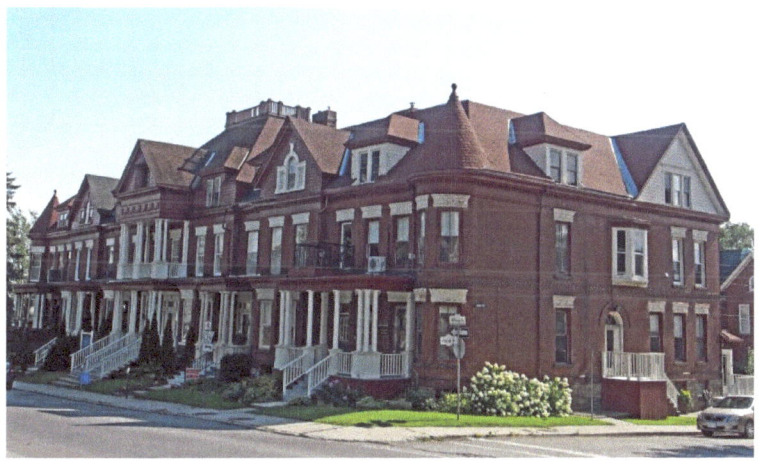

1-6 Court Terrace – Publow Terrace – c. 1895 – Victorian
Romanesque style

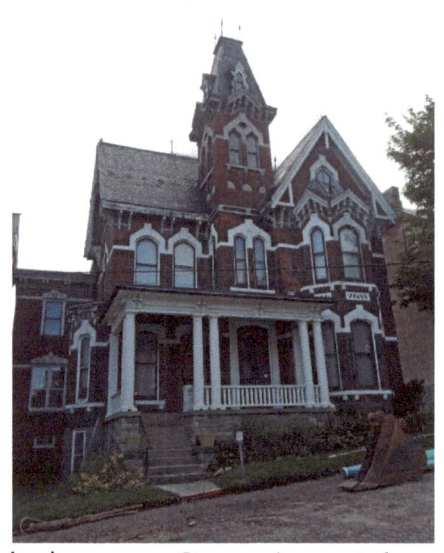

12 Victoria Avenue - Queen Anne style – tower, iron cresting; stone keystones and banding; verge board trim, finials; bay windows; veranda with Doric columns

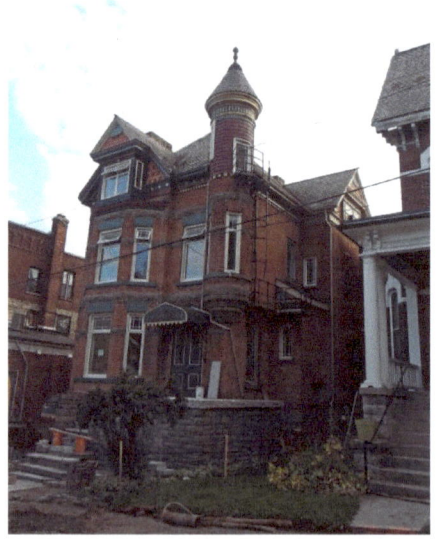

10 Victoria Avenue - Queen Anne style – turret with stone lintels, corbelling and banding; 2-storey bay windows

Architectural Terms

Banding: Different materials, colors or textures used in horizontal bands along a wall. Example: 10 Victoria Avenue, Page 66	
Battlement: A design for a parapet that has alternating solid parts and openings, originally used for defense, but later used as a decorative motif. Example: 144 King Street East, Page 32	
Bay Window: A window that projects out from a wall, in a semicircular, rectangular, or polygonal design. Used frequently in Gothic and Victorian designs. Example: 181 King Street East, Page 36	
Brackets: a decorative or weight-bearing structural element which forms a right angle with one side against a wall and the other under a projecting surface such as an eave or roof. Example: King Street West, Page 18	
Buttress: a masonry structure built against or projecting from a wall which serves to support or reinforce the wall. In Canadian architecture, they are sometimes used for decoration. Example: 10 Church Street, Page 47	

Capital: The uppermost finish or decoration on a column. An Ionic column has a small base, a thin elegant shaft, and a capital composed of volutes which are carved whirls or twists that take the form of a scroll.
Example: 87 King Street West, Page 24
A Doric column is characterized by a plain column with no base, a shaft with twenty flutings, and a simple capital with a simple entablature.
Example: 22 Court House Avenue, Page 12

A Corinthian column is characterized by a rounded capital decorated with acanthus leaves and a square abacus (the uppermost portion of a capital directly below the entablature) on tall slender columns.
Example: Page 42

A Composite is a mixture of two or sometimes, three, of the major styles listed above.
Example: 119 King Street East, Page 28

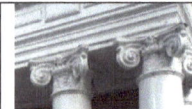
Ionic

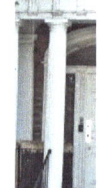
Doric

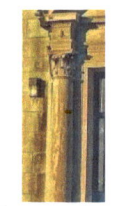
Corinthian

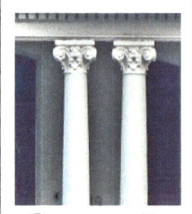
Composite

Corbel: Corbelling is the original method of making arches a series of stones or bricks that protrude beyond the lower level to finally cover the arch. Corbels are used to support cornices, turrets, brackets, ribs and oriel windows. A corbel is also a stone or piece of wood that supports a super incumbent weight.
Example: King Street West, Page 18

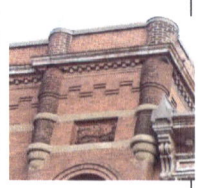

Cornice: originally the wooden overhang of the roof. With the use of stone, brick, iron and steel, the cornice is any horizontal moulded projection at the top of a building. They can be very decorative. Example: King Street West, Page 13	
Cornice Return: decorative element on the end of a gable. Example: King Street East, Page 24	
Course: continuous horizontal row or layer of stone or brick. Example: Page 42	
Cupola: A domed or curved roof rising from a building as a decorative element. Example: 1 King Street East, Page 20	
Dentil Moulding: an even series of rectangles used as ornamental decoration in cornices. Example: 51 King Street West, Page 16	
Dichromatic brickwork: the use of two colors of brick, tile or slate to decorate a façade. Polychromatic is the use of more than two colors. Example: Trinity Anglican Church, Page 61	
Dormer: (French for "sleep") a gable end window that pierces through the plane of a sloping roof surface to create usable space in the top floor or attic of a building by adding headroom. Example: King Street East, Page 23	

Entrance: The entrance encompasses the doorway and the inner vestibule or, in residential architecture, the covered porch. Example: 213 King Street East, Page 38	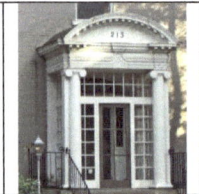
Foil: an architectural device based on a symmetrical rendering of leaf shapes, defined by overlapping circles that produce a series of cusps to make a lobe. The number of cusps can be three (trefoil), four (quatrefoil) or five (cinquefoil), or can be any number (multifoil). Example: 112 King Street East, Page 27	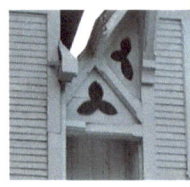 trefoil
Fretwork: interlaced decorative design resembling a bracket Example: 106 Pine Street, Page 64	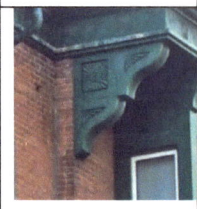
Frontispiece: a portion of the façade of a building, usually a centred doorway that is slightly raised from the rest of the building, usually has extensive ornamentation. Frontispieces are usually Classical in design with white columned porches. Example: Page 40	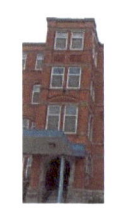
Gable: the triangular portion of a wall between the edges of a sloping roof. Example: 132-140 King Street East, Page 30	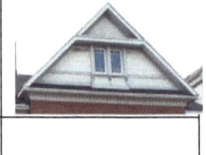
Hip Roof: a roof where all sides slope downwards to the walls with no gables. Example: 196 King Street East, Page 37	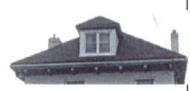

Iron Cresting: a decorative ornament along the top of a roof. Iron cresting was popular in the Baroque era and also in Italianate, Victorian, Second Empire and Queen Anne styles of architecture. Example: 12 Victoria Avenue, Page 66	
Keystones and Voussoirs: a voussoir is a wedge-shaped element used in building an arch. A keystone is the central stone that locks all the stones into position, allowing the arch to bear weight. A keystone is often enlarged and embellished. Example: 149 King Street East, Page 49	
Lancet Window: a tall, narrow window with a pointed arch at its top. Example: 70 King Street East, Page 22	
Lintel: horizontal part above a window or door that supports the structure above it. Example: Church Street, Page 51	
Mansard Roof: This style was popularized by Francois Mansart (1598-1666), an accomplished architect of the French Baroque period and especially fashionable during the Second French Empire (1852-1870). This roof is almost flat on the top section, with two slopes on each of its sides with the lower slope at a steeper angle than the upper and having dormer windows. Example: 181 King Street East, Page 36	

Palladian Window: a large window that is divided into three sections with the centre section larger than the two side sections and usually arched. Example: 165 King Street East, Page 34	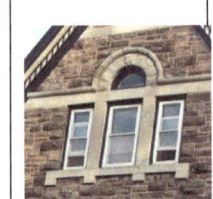
Pediment: a triangular section above the door, or portico, usually supported by columns. The inside of the triangle is called the tympanum. Example: 12-14 Court House Avenue, Page 9	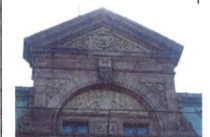
Pilaster: a slightly projecting column built into or applied to the face of a wall for additional structural support. Example: King Street West, Page 13	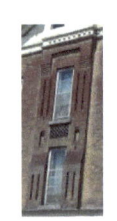
Quoin: masonry blocks at the corner of a wall, often a decorative feature, usually larger or of a different colour than the rest of the wall. Example: 9 Court House Avenue, Page 12	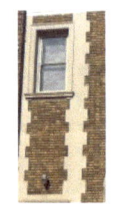
Rose Window: a circular window with ornamental tracery radiating from the centre. Example: 10 Church Street, Page 47	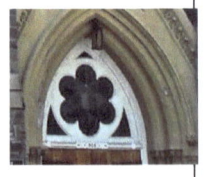

Sidelight: a vertical window that flanks a door, and is often used to emphasize the importance of a primary entrance. **Transom Window:** the light above the doorway, also called a fanlight. Example: 21 Court House Avenue, Page 11	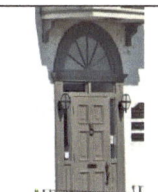
Tower: A circular, square, or octagonal vertical structure higher than the surrounding structure that is usually part of an existing building and is created either for extra defense or for a specific purpose such as a clock or a bell tower. Example: 112 King Street East, Page 27	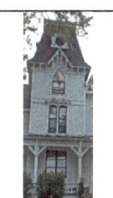
Turret: a small tower that projects from the wall of a building. Example: King Street East, Page 23	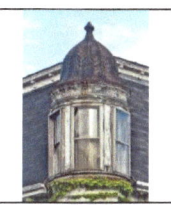
Verge board and Finial: also called bargeboards – hang from the projecting end of a roof and are often elaborately carved and ornamented. Example: 163-165 Church Street, Page 51	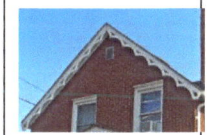
Window Hood: A **hood** is the piece found above window openings, usually of an ornate design, and covers the top third of the opening. Hoods are commonly placed above arched or curved openings on both windows and doors. Example: 181 King Street East, Page 36	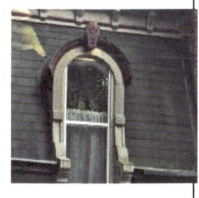

Beaux Arts: Promoters of this style sought to express the classical principles on a grand and imposing scale. Many of the Beaux Arts buildings were banks, post offices, and railway stations. The Ontario Beaux Arts style is eclectic mixing elements of Classical, Renaissance and Baroque. Often the designs have a temple-like façade, porticos with pediments, balustrades, and capitals in many styles. Example: 23 Buell Street, Page 54	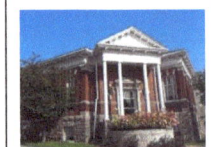
Classical Revival, 1820-1860 – This style was an analytical, scientific, and dogmatic revival based on intensive studies of Greek and Roman buildings, concerned with the application of Greek plans and proportions to civic buildings. Schools, libraries, government offices, and most other civic buildings were built in the Classical Revival style. The white columned porches of the Classical Revival domestic buildings are identified with the mansions of wealthy land owners in Canada. Example: 12-14 Court House Avenue, Page 9	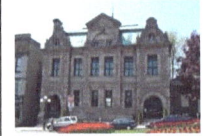
Edwardian, 1900-1930 – This style bridges the ornate and elaborate styles of the Victorian era and the simplified styles of the 20th century. Balanced facades, simple roof lines, dormer windows, large front porches, and smooth brick surfaces are its characteristics. Example: King Street East, Page 24	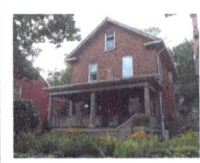

The **Farmhouse** is a country home style that highlights the simplicity of rural living. Comfort and function are the major themes that are associated with the style. The roof frequently flares out to cover the porch. The large porches were designed to help cool the interior of the home and also provide a shady spot for guests to gather and enjoy the outdoors. The architecture is minimally ornamental but very efficient with functional shutters, decorative porch railing, and dormer windows that increase interior light and living space. The exterior is typically faced with horizontal siding. Farmhouse floor plans are usually square or symmetrically shaped, sometimes with side wings. The interior has a large country kitchen and a cluster of bedrooms on the upper level. Farmhouses contain at least one fireplace and large family gathering areas designed for relaxation. Well-crafted and sturdy, farmhouses are generally built to last and withstand for ages.
Example: 301 North Augusta Road, Page 45

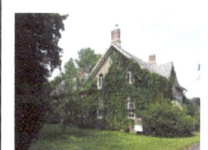

Georgian, before 1860 – This style began with the British King Georges in the 18th century. These buildings have balanced facades around a central door, medium-pitched gable roofs, and small paned windows.
Example: 45 King Street West, Page 17

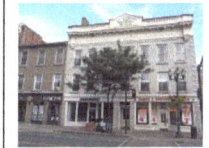

Gothic Revival, 1830-1890 – These decorative buildings have sharply-pitched gables with highly detailed verge boards, pointed-arch window openings, and dichromatic brickwork. It is a common style in Ontario.
Example: 70 King Street East, Page 22

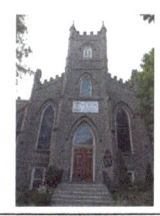

Greek Revival – have gabled or hipped roofs with low pitches. The cornice of the main roof usually has a wide band which represents the entablature of classical Greek architecture consisting of the frieze and the architrave. Greek or Roman columns usually support the porch. The front door is surrounded by sidelights and a rectangular transom and is usually dressed with pilasters, pediments and/or columns. Example: 87 King Street East, Page 24	
Italianate, 1850-1900 – A two story rectangular building with a mild hip roof, a projecting frontispiece, and generous eaves with ornate cornice brackets was the basis of the style; often there are large sash windows, quoins, ornate detailing on the windows, belvederes and wraparound verandahs. Italianate commercial buildings often have cast iron cresting and elegant window surrounds. Example: 126 King Street East, Page 27	
Loyalist style - Timber frame houses with clapboard exterior finishing. In the Loyalist house, the dining room had a fixed position and had particular interior moldings, curtains and detailing to suit it. Fluted pilasters, a large cornice and a plain but prominent architrave were distinct elements of the Loyalist window surround. Example: 12 Church Street, Page 48	

Neo-Classical, 1810-1850 – This style was a direct result of the War of 1812. Many Upper Canadians returning from the war with the United States were second or third generation Loyalists who had inherited land and means from their forefathers. Once the conflict had passed, they had the money and the time to expand their holdings and indulge their architectural whims. Both residential and commercial buildings were constructed on the traditional Georgian plan, but they had a new gaiety and light-heartedness. Detailing became more refined, delicate, and elegant. Example: Court House, Page 6	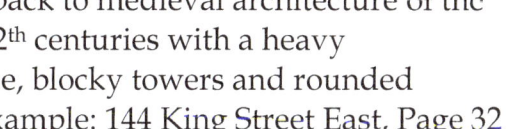
Queen Anne, 1885-1900 – This style is distinguished by an irregular outline featuring a combination of an offset tower, broad gables, projecting two-storey bays, verandahs, multi-sloped roofs, and tall, decorative chimneys. A mixture of brick and wood is common. Windows often have one large single-paned bottom sash and small panes in the upper sash. Example: 152 King Street East, Page 31	
Romanesque Revival, 1880-1910 – This style hearkens back to medieval architecture of the 11th and 12th centuries with a heavy appearance, blocky towers and rounded arches. Example: 144 King Street East, Page 32	

Second Empire, 1860-1880 – The mansard roof is the most noteworthy feature of this style and is evidence of the French origins. Projecting central towers and one or two-storey bays can also be present. Example: King Street East, Page 23	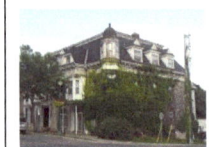
The **Stick style,** 1860-1890 - is named after its use of linear "stickwork" (overlay board strips) on the outside walls to mimic an exposed half-timbered frame. Stick style houses are almost always made with wood. It has a plain layout, often accented with trusses on the gables or decorative shingles. Other characteristics include interpenetrating roof planes with bold paneled brick chimneys, wraparound porch, spindle detailing, the "paneled" sectioning of blank wall, and radiating spindle details at the gable peaks. Example: 112 King Street East, Page 27	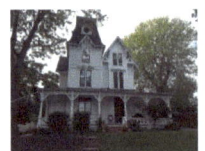
Tudor Revival – exposed timbers with stucco infill, multi-paned windows. Example: 41 Cochrane Drive, Page 46	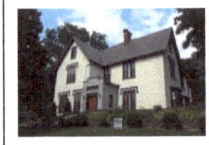
Victorian - In Ontario, a Victorian style building can be seen as any building built between 1840 and 1900 that doesn't fit into any of the other categories. It encompasses a large group of buildings constructed in brick, stone, and timber, using an eclectic mixture of Classical and Gothic motifs. Example: King Street East, Page 37	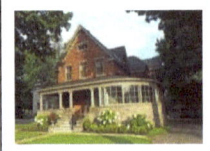

www.ingramcontent.com/pod-product-compliance
Lightning Source LLC
Chambersburg PA
CBHW040831180526
45159CB00001B/147